MW01291348

Legal Notice

BOOKS FROM THE GET 800 COLLECTION FOR COLLEGE BOUND STUDENTS

28 SAT Math Lessons to Improve Your Score in One Month
> Beginner Course
> Intermediate Course
> Advanced Course

New SAT Math Problems arranged by Topic and Difficulty Level
320 SAT Math Problems arranged by Topic and Difficulty Level
SAT Verbal Prep Book for Reading and Writing Mastery
320 SAT Math Subject Test Problems
> Level 1 Test
> Level 2 Test

320 SAT Chemistry Subject Test Problems
Vocabulary Builder
28 ACT Math Lessons to Improve Your Score in One Month
> Advanced Course

320 ACT Math Problems arranged by Topic and Difficulty Level
320 GRE Math Problems arranged by Topic and Difficulty Level
320 AP Calculus AB Problems
320 AP Calculus BC Problems
Physics Mastery for Advanced High School Students
400 SAT Physics Subject Test and AP Physics Problems
SHSAT Verbal Prep Book to Improve Your Score in Two Months
555 Math IQ Questions for Middle School Students
555 Advanced Math Problems for Middle School Students
555 Geometry Problems for High School Students
Algebra Handbook for Gifted Middle School Students
1000 Logic and Reasoning Questions for Gifted and Talented Elementary
> School Students

CONNECT WITH DR. STEVE WARNER

www.facebook.com/SATPrepGet800
www.youtube.com/TheSATMathPrep
www.twitter.com/SATPrepGet800
www.linkedin.com/in/DrSteveWarner
www.pinterest.com/SATPrepGet800
plus.google.com/+SteveWarnerPhD

28 SAT Math
Lessons to Improve Your Score in One Month

Beginner Course

For Students Currently Scoring Below 500
in SAT Math

Dr. Steve Warner

Table of Contents

Actions to Complete Before You Read This Book

1. Purchase a TI-84 or equivalent calculator

It is recommended that you use a TI-84 or comparable calculator for the SAT. Answer explanations in this book will always assume you are using such a calculator.

2. Take a practice SAT from the Official Guide to get your preliminary SAT math score

Your score should be below 500. If it is higher, you can begin with the Intermediate book in this series.

3. Claim your FREE bonuses

Simply visit the following webpage and enter your email address to receive solutions to all the supplemental problems in this book and other materials.

www.thesatmathprep.com/28Les400.html

4. 'Like' my Facebook page

This page is updated regularly with SAT prep advice, tips, tricks, strategies, and practice problems. Visit the following webpage and click the 'like' button.

www.facebook.com/SATPrepGet800

INTRODUCTION
STUDYING FOR SUCCESS

T his book was written specifically for the student currently scoring below a 500 in SAT math. Results will vary, but if you are such a student and you work through the lessons in this book, then you will see a substantial improvement in your score.

This book has been cleverly designed to enforce the study habits that I constantly find students ignoring despite my repeated emphasis on how important they are. Many students will learn and understand the strategies I teach them, but this is not enough. This book will force the student to internalize these strategies so that the appropriate strategy is actually used when it is needed. Most students will attempt the problems that I suggest that they work on, but again, this is not enough. All too often students dismiss errors as "careless" and neglect to redo problems they have answered incorrectly. This book will minimize the effect of this neglect.

The book you are now reading is self-contained. Each lesson was carefully created to ensure that you are making the most effective use of your time while preparing for the SAT. The initial lessons are quite focused ensuring that the reader learns and practices one strategy and one topic at a time. In the beginning the focus is on Level 1 and 2 problems, and little by little Level 3 problems will be added into the mix.

It should be noted that a score of 600 can usually be attained without ever attempting a Level 4 or 5 problem. That said, some Level 4 problems will appear late in the book for those students that show accelerated improvement. The reader should not feel obligated to work on these harder problems the first time they go through this book.

There are two math sections on the SAT: one where a calculator is allowed and one where it is not. I therefore recommend trying to solve as many problems as possible both with and without a calculator. If a calculator is required for a specific problem, it will be marked with an asterisk (*).

1. Using this book effectively

- Begin studying at least three months before the SAT
- Practice SAT math problems ten to fifteen minutes each day
- Choose a consistent study time and location

You will retain much more of what you study if you study in short bursts rather than if you try to tackle everything at once. So, try to choose about a fifteen-minute block of time that you will dedicate to SAT math each day. Make it a habit. The results are well worth this small time commitment. Some students will be able to complete each lesson within this fifteen-minute block of time. Others may take a bit longer. If it takes you longer than fifteen minutes to complete a lesson, you have two options. You can stop when fifteen minutes are up and then complete the lesson the following day, or you can finish the lesson and then take a day off from SAT prep that week.

- Every time you get a question wrong, **mark it off, no matter what your mistake**.
- Begin each lesson by first redoing the problems from previous lessons on the same topic that you have marked off.
- If you get a problem wrong again, **keep it marked off**.

As an example, before you begin the third "Heart of Algebra" lesson (Lesson 9), you should redo all the problems you have marked off from the first two "Heart of Algebra" lessons (Lessons 1 and 5). Any question that you get right you can "unmark" while leaving questions that you get wrong marked off for the next time. If this takes you the full fifteen minutes, that is okay. Just begin the new lesson the next day.

Note that this book often emphasizes solving each problem in more than one way. Please listen to this advice. The same question is never repeated on any SAT (with the exception of questions from the experimental sections) so the important thing is learning as many techniques as possible. Being able to solve any specific problem is of minimal importance. The more ways you have to solve a single problem the more prepared you will be to tackle a problem you have never seen before, and the quicker you will be able to solve that problem. Also, if you have multiple methods for solving a single problem, then on the actual SAT when you "check over" your work you will be able to redo each problem in a different way. This will eliminate all "careless" errors on the actual exam. Note that in this book the quickest solution to any problem will always be marked with an asterisk (*).

2.   Calculator use.

- Use a TI-84 or comparable calculator if possible when practicing and during the SAT.
- Make sure that your calculator has fresh batteries on test day.
- You may have to switch between DEGREE and RADIAN modes during the test. If you are using a TI-84 (or equivalent) calculator press the MODE button and scroll down to the third line when necessary to switch between modes.

Below are the most important things you should practice on your graphing calculator.

- Practice entering complicated computations in a single step.
- Know when to insert parentheses:
    - Around numerators of fractions
    - Around denominators of fractions
    - Around exponents
    - Whenever you actually see parentheses in the expression

Examples:

We will substitute a 5 in for x in each of the following examples.

Expression	Calculator computation
$\dfrac{7x+3}{2x-11}$	$(7*5 + 3)/(2*5 - 11)$
$(3x-8)^{2x-9}$	$(3*5 - 8)\wedge(2*5 - 9)$

9

- Clear the screen before using it in a new problem. The big screen allows you to check over your computations easily.
- Press the **ANS** button (**2ⁿᵈ (-)**) to use your last answer in the next computation.
- Press **2ⁿᵈ ENTER** to bring up your last computation for editing. This is especially useful when you are plugging in answer choices, or guessing and checking.
- You can press **2ⁿᵈ ENTER** over and over again to cycle backwards through all the computations you have ever done.
- Know where the $\sqrt{}$, π , and ∧ buttons are so you can reach them quickly.
- Change a decimal to a fraction by pressing **MATH ENTER ENTER**.
- Press the **MATH** button - in the first menu that appears you can take cube roots and nth roots for any n. Scroll right to **NUM** and you have **lcm(** and **gcd(**.
- Know how to use the **SIN**, **COS** and **TAN** buttons as well as **SIN⁻¹**, **COS⁻¹** and **TAN⁻¹**.

3. Tips for taking the SAT

Each of the following tips should be used whenever you take a practice SAT as well as on the actual exam.

Check your answers properly: When you go back to check your earlier answers for careless errors *do not* simply look over your work to try to catch a mistake. This is usually a waste of time.

- When "checking over" problems you have already done, **always redo the problem from the beginning** without looking at your earlier work.
- If possible, use a different method than you used the first time.

For example, if you solved the problem by picking numbers the first time, try a different method, or at least pick different numbers the second time. Always do the problem from the beginning and do not look at your original solution. If your two answers do not match up, then you know that this is a problem you need to spend a little more time on to figure out where your error is.

This may seem time consuming, but that is okay. It is better to spend more time checking over a few problems, than to rush through a lot of problems and repeat the same mistakes.

Take a guess whenever you cannot solve a problem: There is no guessing penalty on the SAT. Whenever you do not know how to solve a problem take a guess. Ideally you should eliminate as many answer choices as possible before taking your guess, but if you have no idea whatsoever do not waste time overthinking. Simply put down an answer and move on. You should certainly mark it off and come back to it later if you have time.

Pace yourself: Do not waste your time on a question that is too hard or will take too long. After you have been working on a question for about 1 minute you need to make a decision. If you understand the question and think that you can get the answer within another minute or so, continue to work on the problem. If you still do not know how to do the problem or you are using a technique that is going to take a long time, mark it off and come back to it later if you have time.

Feel free to take a guess. But you still want to leave open the possibility of coming back to it later. Remember that every problem is worth the same amount. Do not sacrifice problems that you may be able to do by getting hung up on a problem that is too hard for you.

Attempt the right number of questions: There are two math sections on the SAT – one where a calculator is allowed and one where a calculator is not allowed. The calculator section has 30 multiple choice (mc) questions and 8 free response (grid in) questions. The non-calculator section has 15 multiple choice (mc) questions and 5 free response (grid in) questions.

You should first make sure that you know what you got on your last SAT practice test, actual SAT, or actual PSAT (whichever you took last). What follows is a general goal you should go for when taking the exam.

Score	MC (Calculator Allowed)	Grid In (Calculator Allowed)	MC (Calculator Not Allowed)	Grid In (Calculator Not Allowed)
< 330	10/30	3/8	4/15	1/5
330 – 370	15/30	4/8	6/15	2/5
380 – 430	18/30	5/8	8/15	2/5
440 – 490	21/30	6/8	9/15	3/5
500 – 550	24/30	6/8	11/15	4/5
560 – 620	27/30	7/8	13/15	4/5
630 – 800	30/30	8/8	15/15	5/5

For example, a student with a current score of 420 should attempt 18 multiple choice questions and 5 grid ins from the section where a calculator is allowed, and 8 multiple choice questions and 2 grid in questions from the section where a calculator is not allowed.

This is *just* a general guideline. Of course, it can be fine-tuned. As a simple example, if you are particularly strong at Algebra problems, but very weak at Geometry and Trig problems, then you may want to try every Algebra problem no matter where it appears, and you may want to reduce the number of Geometry and Trig problems you attempt.

Grid your answers correctly: The computer only grades what you have marked in the bubbles. The space above the bubbles is just for your convenience, and to help you do your bubbling correctly.

Never mark more than one circle in a column or the problem will automatically be marked wrong. You do not need to use all four columns. If you do not use a column just leave it blank.

The symbols that you can grid in are the digits 0 through 9, a decimal point, and a division symbol for fractions. Note that there is no negative symbol. So, answers to grid-ins *cannot* be negative. Also, there are only four slots, so you cannot get an answer such as 52,326.

12

Sometimes there is more than one correct answer to a grid-in question. Simply choose one of them to grid-in. *Never* try to fit more than one answer into the grid.

If your answer is a whole number such as 2451 or a decimal that only requires four or less slots such as 2.36, then simply enter the number starting at any column. The two examples just written must be started in the first column, but the number 16 can be entered starting in column 1, 2 or 3.

Note that there is no zero in column 1, so if your answer is 0 it must be gridded into column 2, 3 or 4.

Fractions can be gridded in any form as long as there are enough slots. The fraction 2/100 must be reduced to 1/50 simply because the first representation will not fit in the grid.

Fractions can also be converted to decimals before being gridded in. If a decimal cannot fit in the grid, then you can simply *truncate* it to fit. But you must use every slot in this case. For example, the decimal .167777777... can be gridded as .167, but .16 or .17 would both be marked wrong.

Instead of truncating decimals you can also *round* them. For example, the decimal above could be gridded as .168. Truncating is preferred because there is no thinking involved and you are less likely to make a careless error.

Here are three ways to grid in the number 8/9.

Never grid-in mixed numerals. If your answer is $2\frac{1}{4}$, and you grid in the mixed numeral $2\frac{1}{4}$, then this will be read as 21/4 and will be marked wrong. You must either grid in the decimal 2.25 or the improper fraction 9/4.

Here are two ways to grid in the mixed numeral $1\frac{1}{2}$ correctly.

LESSON 1
HEART OF ALGEBRA

Start with Choice (B) or (C)

In many SAT math problems, you can get the answer simply by trying each of the answer choices until you find the one that works. Unless you have some intuition as to what the correct answer might be, then you should always start in the middle with choice (B) or (C) as your first guess (an exception will be detailed in the next strategy below). The reason for this is simple. Answers are usually given in increasing or decreasing order. So very often if choice (B) or (C) fails you can eliminate one or two of the other choices as well.

Try to answer the following question using this strategy. **Do not** check the solution until you have attempted this question yourself.

LEVEL 1: ALGEBRA

1. If $2^{3y} = 64$, then $y =$

    (A) 3
    (B) 2
    (C) 1
    (D) 0

Solution by starting with choice (C): Begin by looking at choice (C). We substitute 1 in for y on the left-hand side of the given equation to get $2^{3y} = 2^{3 \cdot 1} = 2^3 = 2 \cdot 2 \cdot 2 = 8$. This is too small. So, we can eliminate choices (C) and (D).

Let's try choice (B) next. We substitute 2 in for y on the left-hand side of the equation to get $2^{3y} = 2^{3 \cdot 2} = 2^6 = 2 \cdot 2 \cdot 2 \cdot 2 \cdot 2 \cdot 2 = 64$. This is correct so that the answer is choice (B).

Remarks: (1) If allowed you should do the above computations with your TI-84 calculator. To compute $2^{3 \cdot 2}$ you can either type 2^(3*2) or 2^6 in your calculator. Note that if you use the first option, it is **essential** that you put parentheses around 3*2.

(2) If you type 2^3*2 in your calculator, you will get the **incorrect** answer of 16. This is because your calculator does 2^3 first, and then multiplies by 2. This is **not** what you want.

Before we go on, try to solve this problem algebraically.

* **Algebraic solution:** $64 = 2 \cdot 2 \cdot 2 \cdot 2 \cdot 2 \cdot 2 = 2^6$. So, replacing 64 by 2^6 in the given equation, we have $2^{3y} = 2^6$. So $3y = 6$, and therefore $y = 2$, choice (B).

Remark: To see that $64 = 2^6$ we can simply use trial and error and our calculator if a calculator is allowed.

If a calculator is not allowed, we can count how many times we need to multiply 2 by itself to get to 64.

Informal and Formal Algebra

Suppose we are asked to solve for x in the following equation:

$$x + 3 = 8$$

In other words, we are being asked for a number such that when we add 3 to that number we get 8. It is not too hard to see that $5 + 3 = 8$, so that $x = 5$.

I call the technique above solving this equation **informally**. In other words, when we solve algebraic equations informally we are solving for the variable very quickly in our heads. I sometimes call this performing **"mental math."**

We can also solve for x **formally** by subtracting 3 from each side of the equation:

$$
\begin{array}{r}
x + 3 = 8 \\
\underline{-3 \quad -3} \\
x \quad\ \ = 5
\end{array}
$$

In other words, when we solve an algebraic equation formally we are writing out all the steps – just as we would do it on a test in school.

To save time on the SAT you should practice solving equations informally as much as possible. And you should also practice solving equations formally – this will increase your mathematical skill level.

16

Let's try another:

$$5x = 30$$

Informally, 5 times 6 is 30, so we see that $x = 6$.

Formally, we can divide each side of the equation by 5:

$$\frac{5x}{5} = \frac{30}{5}$$
$$x = 6$$

Now let's get a little harder:

$$5x + 3 = 48$$

We can still do this informally. First let's figure out what number plus 3 is 48. Well, 45 plus 3 is 48. So $5x$ is 45. So x must be 9.

Here is the formal solution:

$$5x + 3 = 48$$
$$\underline{-3 \quad -3}$$
$$\frac{5x}{5} \quad = \frac{45}{5}$$
$$x \quad = 9$$

Now try to solve each of the following problems by starting with choice (B) or (C). Then, if possible, solve each problem algebraically (either informally or formally). The answers to these problems, followed by full solutions are at the end of this lesson. **Do not** look at the answers until you have attempted these problems yourself. Please remember to mark off any problems you get wrong.

LEVEL 1: ALGEBRA

$$\frac{9 + \Delta}{2} = 9\frac{1}{2}$$

2. What number, when used in place of Δ above, makes the statement true?

   (A) 4
   (B) 5
   (C) 10
   (D) 12

3. If $8 + x + x = 4 + x + x + x$, what is the value of x ?

    (A) 1
    (B) 2
    (C) 3
    (D) 4

4. If $5(x - 7) = 4(x - 8)$, what is the value of x ?

    (A) 1
    (B) 2
    (C) 3
    (D) 4

LEVEL 2: ALGEBRA

5. * If $4^{x+1} = 4096$, what is the value of x ?

    (A) 6
    (B) 5
    (C) 4
    (D) 3

6. If $(x - 3)^2 = 36$, and $x < 0$, what is the value of x ?

    (A) -33
    (B) -9
    (C) -3
    (D) -2

Answers

1. B	4. C
2. C	5. B
3. D	6. C

Full Solutions

2.
Solution by starting with choice (C): Begin by looking at choice (C). We substitute 10 in for Δ in the given equation.

$$\frac{9 + 10}{2} = 9\frac{1}{2}$$

$$\frac{19}{2} = 9\frac{1}{2}$$

$$9\frac{1}{2} = 9\frac{1}{2}$$

The equation is true. So the answer is choice (C).

* Algebraic solution:

$$\frac{9 + \Delta}{2} = 9\frac{1}{2}$$

$$9 + \Delta = 19$$

$$\Delta = 10$$

This is choice (C).

3.

Solution by starting with choice (C): Begin by looking at choice (C). We substitute 3 in for x on each side of the equation.

$$8 + 3 + 3 = 4 + 3 + 3 + 3$$

$$14 = 13$$

Since this is false, we can eliminate choice (C). A little thought should allow you to eliminate choices (A) and (B) as well (don't worry if you don't see this – just take another guess). Let's try choice (D) next.

$$8 + 4 + 4 = 4 + 4 + 4 + 4$$

$$16 = 16$$

Thus, the answer is choice (D).

Algebraic solution:

$$8 + x + x = 4 + x + x + x$$

$$8 + 2x = 4 + 3x$$

$$8 = 4 + x$$

$$4 = x$$

Thus, the answer is choice (D).

Remark: We can begin with an algebraic solution, and then switch to the easier method. For example, we can write $7 + 2x = 3 + 3x$, and then start substituting in the answer choices from here. This will take less time than the first method, but more time than the algebraic method.

* Striking off x's: When the same term appears on each side of an equation we can simply delete that term from both sides. In this problem, we can strike off two x's from each side to get

$$8 = 4 + x.$$

This becomes $4 = x$, choice (D).

   4.
Solution by starting with choice (C): Begin by looking at choice (C). We substitute 3 in for x in the given equation.

$$5(x - 7) = 4(x - 8)$$
$$5(3 - 7) = 4(3 - 8)$$
$$5(-4) = 4(-5)$$
$$-20 = -20$$

Thus, the answer is choice (C).

* Algebraic solution:
$$5(x - 7) = 4(x - 8)$$
$$5x - 35 = 4x - 32$$
$$x = 3$$

Thus, the answer is choice (C).

   5.
Solution by starting with choice (C): Begin by looking at choice (C). We substitute 4 in for x in the given equation. We type in our calculator $4\string^(4 + 1) = 1024$. This is too small so we can eliminate choices (C) and (D). Let's try choice (B) next.

We type in our calculator $4\string^(5 + 1) = 4096$. This is correct. Thus, the answer is choice (B).

Calculator notes: (1) If you find yourself getting the wrong answer when you use your calculator, please review (1) under Calculator Use on page 9.

(2) Instead of typing 4^(4 + 1) in our calculator, we can add 4 and 1 in our head (to get 5), and type 4^5 instead. Similarly, we can type 4^6 instead of 4^(5 + 1).

* Algebraic solution: We rewrite the equation so that each side has the same base (in this case the common base is 4). $4^{x+1} = 4^6$. Now that the bases are the same, so are the exponents. Thus, $x + 1 = 6$, and therefore $x = 5$, choice (B).

6.

Solution by starting with choice (C): Let's guess that choice (C) is the answer and let $x = -3$. Then $(x - 3)^2 = (-3 - 3)^2 = (-6)^2 = 36$. This is correct. So the answer is choice (C).

Remark: The square of a number is **always** nonnegative. As an example, $(-6)^2 = 36$ and **not** -36. Compare this to -6^2 which is equal to $(-1)(6^2) = (-1)(36) = -36$.

Order of Operations: A quick review of order of operations.

PEMDAS	
P	Parentheses
E	Exponentiation
M	Multiplication
D	Division
A	Addition
S	Subtraction

Note that multiplication and division have the same priority, and addition and subtraction have the same priority.

* Algebraic solution: We use the **square root property**, and then solve for x.

$$(x - 3)^2 = 36$$
$$x - 3 = \pm 6$$
$$x = 3 \pm 6$$
$$x = 3 - 6 \text{ or } x = 3 + 6$$
$$x = -3 \text{ or } x = 9$$

Since it is given that $x < 0$, the answer is $x = -3$, choice (C).

Remark: The **square root property** says that if $b^2 = a$, then $b = \pm\sqrt{a}$.

Common Error: When solving an equation with a "square" in it students will often apply the square root property incorrectly by taking only the positive square root. In this problem, the erroneous computation might look like this.

$$(x - 3)^2 = 36$$
$$x - 3 = 6$$
$$x = 9$$

This is not one of the answer choices, but nonetheless many students will choose choice (B) because it looks similar. DO NOT fall into this trap!

OPTIONAL MATERIAL

Try to solve each of the following equations for x both informally, and formally. The answers are below:

1. $x + 17 = 20$
2. $6x = 24$
3. $\dfrac{x}{12} = 2$
4. $7x - 4 = 24$
5. $\dfrac{2x-3}{5} = 2$

6. $5(x - 7) = 40$
7. $2^x = 8$
8. $\dfrac{5+x}{2} = 8\dfrac{1}{2}$
9. $5^{x+1} = 125$
10. $3^x + 4 = 31$

Answers

1. 3
2. 4
3. 24
4. 4
5. 13/2 or 6.5

6. 15
7. 3
8. 12
9. 2
10. 3

LESSON 2
GEOMETRY

Triangles

A **triangle** is a two-dimensional geometric figure with three sides and three angles. The sum of the degree measures of all three angles of a triangle is 180.

A triangle is **acute** if all three of its angles measure less than 90 degrees. A triangle is **obtuse** if one angle has a measure greater than 90 degrees. A triangle is **right** if it has one angle that measures exactly 90 degrees.

Example 1:

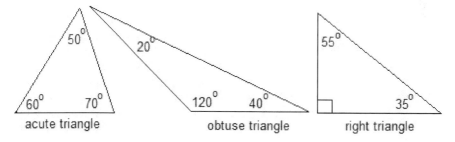

acute triangle   obtuse triangle   right triangle

A triangle is **isosceles** if it has two sides of equal length. Equivalently, an isosceles triangle has two angles of equal measure.

A triangle is **equilateral** if all three of its sides have equal length. Equivalently, an equilateral triangle has three angles of equal measure (all three angles measure 60 degrees).

Example 2:

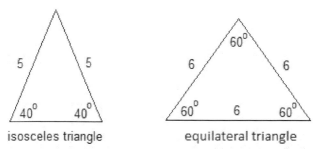

isosceles triangle   equilateral triangle

23

Quadrilaterals

A **quadrilateral** is a two-dimensional geometric figure with four sides and four angles. The sum of the degree measures of all four angles of a quadrilateral is 360.

A **rectangle** is a quadrilateral in which each angle is a right angle. That is, each angle measures 90 degrees.

The **perimeter** of a rectangle is $P = 2\ell + 2w$, and the area of a rectangle is $A = \ell w$.

A **square** is a rectangle with four equal sides. The area of a square is $A = s^2$.

Example 3:

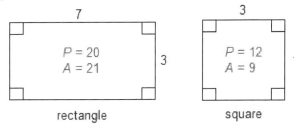

Turn to page 15 and review **Start with choice (B) or (C)**. Then try to answer the following question using this strategy. **Do not** check the solution until you have attempted this question yourself.

LEVEL 1: GEOMETRY

1. If the degree measures of the three angles of a triangle are 40°, $z°$, and $z°$, what is the value of z ?

   (A) 100
   (B) 90
   (C) 80
   (D) 70

Solution by starting with choice (C): Recall that a triangle has angle measures that sum to 180 degrees.

Let us start with choice (C) and guess that $z = 80$. Then the sum of the measures of the angles is equal to $40 + z + z = 40 + 80 + 80 = 200°$.

This is too large. We can therefore eliminate choices (A), (B), and (C). So, the answer is choice (D).

Note: Let us just verify that choice (D) is in fact the answer. So, we are guessing that $z = 70$. It follows that the sum of the angle measures is $40 + z + z = 40 + 70 + 70 = 180°$. Since this is correct, the answer is choice (D).

Before we go on, try to solve this problem algebraically.

* Algebraic solution: Since the angle measures of a triangle sum to 180 degrees, we solve the following equation.

$$40 + z + z = 180$$
$$40 + 2z = 180$$
$$2z = 140$$
$$z = 70$$

Therefore, the answer is choice (D).

You're doing great! Let's just practice a bit more. Try to solve each of the following problems by starting with choice (B) or (C). Then, if possible, solve each problem another way. The answers to these problems, followed by full solutions are at the end of this lesson. **Do not** look at the answers until you have attempted these problems yourself. Please remember to mark off any problems you get wrong.

LEVEL 1: GEOMETRY

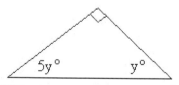

Note: Figure not drawn to scale.

2.   In the right triangle above, what is the value of y ?

    (A) 15
    (B) 18
    (C) 21
    (D) 30

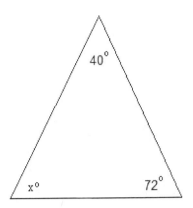

3. In the triangle above, $x=$

    (A) 62
    (B) 64
    (C) 66
    (D) 68

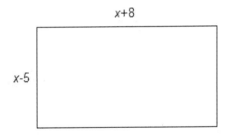

4. If the perimeter of the rectangle above is 78, what is the value of x?

    (A) 20
    (B) 19
    (C) 18
    (D) 17

26

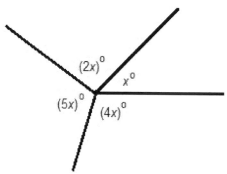

Note: Figure not drawn to scale.

5. In the figure above, four line segments meet at a point to form four angles. What is the value of x?

    (A) 18
    (B) 24
    (C) 30
    (D) 40

Answers

1. D	4. C
2. A	5. C
3. D	

Full Solutions

2.

Solution by starting with choice (C): Recall that a triangle has angle measures that sum to 180 degrees, and begin by looking at choice (C). So we let $y = 21$. Then $5y = (5)(21) = 105$.

$$90 + 21 + 105 = 216.$$

Since $216 > 180$ we can eliminate choice (C), as well as choice (D).

Let's try choice (A) next. So, we let $y = 15$. Then $5y = (5)(15) = 75$.

$$90 + 15 + 75 = 180.$$

Therefore, choice (A) is the correct answer.

* **Algebraic solution:** $5y + y$ must be equal to 90. So $6y = 90$, and therefore $y = \dfrac{90}{6} = 15$, choice (A).

3.

Solution by starting with choice (C): Recall that a triangle has angle measures that sum to 180 degrees, and begin by looking at choice (C). If we let $x = 66$, then $66 + 40 + 72 = 178$. This is a bit too small, so we can eliminate choices (A), (B), and (C). So, the answer is choice (D).

* **Algebraic solution:** We solve the following equation.

$$x + 40 + 72 = 180$$
$$x + 112 = 180$$
$$x = 68$$

This is answer choice (D).

4.

Solution by starting with choice (C): Recall that we get the **perimeter** of a rectangle by adding up all four sides. Let's start with choice (C) as our first guess, so that $x = 18$. Then we have $x - 5 = 18 - 5 = 13$ and $x + 8 = 18 + 8 = 26$. So, the perimeter is $13 + 13 + 26 + 26 = 78$. Therefore, the answer is choice (C).

Algebraic solution: We solve the following equation.

$$P = 2l + 2w$$
$$78 = 2(x + 8) + 2(x - 5)$$
$$78 = 2x + 16 + 2x - 10$$
$$78 = 4x + 6$$
$$72 = 4x$$
$$\frac{72}{4} = x$$
$$18 = x$$

This is answer choice (C).

5.

First note that the measures of the four angles must add up to 360 degrees. We can now proceed in two ways.

Method 1- Starting with choice (C): Let's start with choice (C) and guess that $x = 30$. Then

$$30 + 2(30) + 4(30) + 5(30) = 30 + 60 + 120 + 150 = 360.$$

This is correct so that the answer is choice (C).

* **Method 2 – Algebraic solution:** $x + 2x + 4x + 5x = 12x$. So, $12x = 360$, and therefore $x = \dfrac{360}{12} = 30$, choice (C).

OPTIONAL MATERIAL

The following question will test your understanding of formulas used in this lesson. This is **not** an SAT question.

1. Find the perimeter and area of a rectangle with each of the following lengths and widths.

$\ell = 3, w = 5$ $\ell = 2.3, w = 1.7$ $\ell = x - 2, w = x + 3$ $\ell = x - 4, w = x^2 + 5$

Answers

1. $P = 16$, $A = 15$; $P = 8$, $A = 3.91$; $P = 4x + 2$, $A = (x - 2)(x + 3) = x^2 + x - 6$; $P = 2x^2 + 2x + 2$, $A = (x - 4)(x^2 + 5) = x^3 - 4x^2 + 5x - 20$

LESSON 3
PASSPORT TO ADVANCED MATH

Functions

A function is simply a rule that for each "input" assigns a specific "output." Functions may be given by equations, tables or graphs.

Note about the notation $f(x)$: The variable x is a placeholder. We evaluate the function f at a specific value by substituting that value in for x. For example, if $f(x) = 2x^2 + x - 1$, then

$$f(3) = 2(3)^2 + 3 - 1 = 2 \cdot 9 + 2 = 18 + 2 = \mathbf{20}.$$

LEVEL 1: ADVANCED MATH

$$f(x) = x^2 + 1$$
$$g(x) = 2x - 3$$

1. The functions f and g are defined above. What is the value of $g(5) - f(1)$?

* Solution: $g(5) = 2(5) - 3 = 10 - 3 = 7$.

$f(1) = 1^2 + 1 = 1 + 1 = 2$.

Therefore $g(5) - f(1) = 7 - 2 = \mathbf{5}$.

Turn to page 15 and review **Start with choice (B) or (C)**. Then try to answer the following question using this strategy. **Do not** check the solution until you have attempted this question yourself.

LEVEL 1: ADVANCED MATH

2. If $2k^2 - 17 = 31 - k^2$, what are all possible values of k?

(A) 4 only
(B) −4 only
(C) 0 only
(D) 4 and −4 only

30

Solution by starting with choice (C): Let's start with choice (C) and try $k = 0$.

$k = 0$: $2(0)^2 - 17 = 31 - 0^2$ $-17 = 31$

Since this is False we can eliminate choice (C).

Based on the remaining answer choices it seems that we will need to check both 4 and -4.

$k = 4$: $2(4)^2 - 17 = 31 - 4^2$ $15 = 15$ True

$k = -4$: $2(-4)^2 - 17 = 31 - (-4)^2$ $15 = 15$ True

Since the equation is true for both $k = 4$ and $k = -4$, the answer is (D).

Notes: (1) Since all powers of k in the given equation are even, 4 and -4 must give the same answer. So, we didn't really need to check -4.

(2) Observe that when performing the computations above, the proper order of operations was followed. Exponentiation was done first, followed by multiplication, and then subtraction was done last.

For example, we have $2(4)^2 - 17 = 2 \cdot 16 - 17 = 32 - 17 = 15$ and $31 - 4^2 = 31 - 16 = 15$.

See the solution to problem 6 in Lesson 1 for a review of order of operations.

Also, try to solve this problem algebraically.

* Algebraic solution: We add k^2 to each side of the given equation to get $3k^2 - 17 = 31$. We then add 17 to get $3k^2 = 31 + 17 = 48$. Dividing each side of this last equation by 3 gives $k^2 = \frac{48}{3} = 16$. We now use the **square root property** to get $k = \pm 4$. So, the answer is choice (D).

Notes: (1) The equation $k^2 = 16$ has two solutions: $k = 4$ and $k = -4$. A common mistake is to forget about the negative solution.

(2) The **square root property** says that if $x^2 = c$, then $x = \pm\sqrt{c}$.

This is different from taking the positive square root of a number. For example, $\sqrt{16} = 4$, whereas the equation $x^2 = 16$ has two solutions $x = \pm 4$.

(3) Another way to solve the equation $k^2 = 16$ is to subtract 16 from each side of the equation, and then factor the difference of two squares as follows:

$$k^2 - 16 = 0$$
$$(k - 4)(k + 4) = 0$$

We now set each factor equal to 0 to get $k - 4 = 0$ or $k + 4 = 0$.

So $k = 4$ or $k = -4$.

Now try to answer the following questions. Use the strategy of starting with choice (B) or (C) whenever possible. Also, try to solve each problem another way. The answers to these questions, followed by full solutions are at the end of this lesson. **Do not** look at the answers until you have attempted these problems yourself. Please remember to mark off any problems you get wrong.

LEVEL 1: ADVANCED MATH

3. For the function $f(x) = 3x^2 - x$, what is the value of $f(-2)$?

x	$p(x)$	$q(x)$	$r(x)$
1	5	6	11
2	3	7	10
3	4	3	7
4	5	7	2
5	6	1	5

4. The table above gives some values of the functions p, q, and r. At which value of x does $q(x) = p(x) + r(x)$?

LEVEL 2: ADVANCED MATH

$$h(x) = |x^2 - 3| + 2$$

5. For what value of x is $h(x)$ equal to 0?

    (A) 0
    (B) 1
    (C) $\sqrt{3}$
    (D) There is no such value of x

6. Suppose that $h(x) = x^2 + 1$ and $h(b) = 26$. What is a possible value of b?

    (A) 4
    (B) 5
    (C) 6
    (D) 6.5

Answers

1. 5	4. 4
2. D	5. D
3. 14	6. B

Full Solutions

3.
* $f(-2) = 3(-2)^2 - (-2) = 3(4) + 2 = 12 + 2 = \mathbf{14}$.

Notes: (1) The exponentiation was done first, followed by the multiplication. Addition was done last. See the solution to problem 6 in Lesson 1 for a review of order of operations.

(2) To square a number means to multiply it by itself. So

$$(-2)^2 = (-2)(-2) = 4.$$

(3) If a calculator is allowed, we can do the whole computation in our calculator in one step. Simply type 3(−2)^2 − (−2) ENTER. The output will be 14.

Make sure to use the minus sign and not the subtraction symbol in front of the 2. Otherwise the calculator will give an error.

4.

* Solution by starting with 3: The answer is an integer between 1 and 5 inclusive (these are the x-values given). So, let's start with $x = 3$ as our first guess. From the table $p(3) = 4$, $q(3) = 3$, and $r(3) = 7$. Therefore $p(3) + r(3) = 4 + 7 = 11$. This is not equal to $q(3)$ so that 3 is **not** the answer.

Let's try $x = 4$ next. From the table $p(4) = 5$, $q(4) = 7$, and $r(4) = 2$. So $p(4) + r(4) = 5 + 2 = 7 = q(4)$. Therefore, the answer is **4**.

* Quick solution: We can just glance at the rows quickly and observe that in the row corresponding to $x = 4$, we have $5 + 2 = 7$. Thus, the answer is **4**.

5.

Solution by starting with choice (C): We start with choice (C) and compute $h(\sqrt{3}) = |(\sqrt{3})^2 - 3| + 2 = |3 - 3| + 2 = 0 + 2 = 2$.

So, we can eliminate choice (C).

Let's try (B): $h(1) = |1^2 - 3| + 2 = |1 - 3| + 2 = |-2| + 2 = 4$.

So, we can eliminate choice (B).

Let's try (A): $h(0) = |-3| + 2 = 3 + 2 = 5$.

So, we can eliminate choice (A) and the answer is choice (D).

* Direct solution: $|x^2 - 3| \geq 0$ no matter what x is. It follows that $|x^2 - 3| + 2 \geq 2$.

In particular, $|x^2 - 3| + 2$ could never be 0, and so the answer is (D).

Recall: $|x|$ is the **absolute value** of x. If x is nonnegative, then $|x| = x$. If x is negative, then $|x| = -x$ (in other words, if x is negative, then taking the absolute value just eliminates the minus sign). For example, $|12| = 12$ and $|-12| = 12$.

6.

Solution by starting with choice (C): Let's start with choice (C) and guess that $b = 6$. Then $h(b) = 6^2 + 1 = 36 + 1 = 37$. This is too big. So we can eliminate choices (C) and (D).

Let's try choice (B) next. So, we are guessing that $b = 5$. We then have that $h(b) = 5^2 + 1 = 25 + 1 = 26$. This is correct. So, the answer is choice (B).

* **Algebraic solution:** $h(b) = 26$ is equivalent to $b^2 + 1 = 26$. We subtract 1 from each side of this equation to get $b^2 = 25$. So, a possible value of b is 5, choice (B).

Note: As in problem 2, the square root property gives two solutions to the equation $b^2 = 25$. What are these two solutions? Can you also solve this equation by factoring? See the notes after the algebraic solution to problem 2 for details.

Download additional solutions for free here:

www.thesatmathprep.com/28Les400.html

LESSON 4
STATISTICS

Basic Statistics

The **average (arithmetic mean)** of a list of numbers is the sum of the numbers in the list divided by the quantity of the numbers in the list.

$$\textbf{Average} = \frac{\textbf{Sum}}{\textbf{Number}}$$

The **median** of a list of numbers is the middle number when the numbers are arranged in increasing order. If the total number of values in the list is even, then the median is the average of the two middle values.

Example 1: Let's compute the average (arithmetic mean) and median of 1, 5, 6, 8, 10

$$\text{Average} = \frac{1+5+6+8+10}{5} = \frac{30}{5} = \textbf{6} \qquad \text{Median} = \textbf{6}$$

Example 2: Let's compute the average (arithmetic mean) and median of 7, 2, 5, 18, 10, 3

$$\text{Average} = \frac{7+2+5+18+10+3}{6} = \frac{45}{6} = \textbf{7.5}$$

To find the median it is helpful to rewrite the numbers in increasing order: 2, 3, 5, 7, 10, 18. Then the median is $\frac{5+7}{2} = \frac{12}{2} = \textbf{6}$.

Change Averages to Sums

A problem involving averages often becomes much easier when we first convert the averages to sums. We can easily change an average to a sum using the following simple formula.

Sum = Average · Number

Many problems with averages involve one or more conversions to sums, followed by a subtraction.

Note: The above formula comes from eliminating the denominator in the definition of average.

$$\textbf{Average} = \frac{\textbf{Sum}}{\textbf{Number}}$$

Try to answer the following question using this strategy. **Do not** check the solution until you have attempted this question yourself.

LEVEL 1: STATISTICS

1. The average (arithmetic mean) of three numbers is 80. If two of the numbers are 70 and 85, what is the third number?

   (A) 75
   (B) 80
   (C) 85
   (D) 90

* Solution by changing averages to sums: In this case, we are averaging 3 numbers. Thus, the **Number** is 3. The **Average** is given to be 80. So, the **Sum** of the 3 numbers is $80 \cdot 3 = 240$. Since we know that two of the numbers are 70 and 85, the third number is $240 - 70 - 85 = 85$, choice (C).

Before we go on, try to solve this problem in two other ways.

(1) By "Starting with Choice (C)."

(2) Algebraically (the way you would do it in school).

Solution by starting with choice (C): Let's start with choice (C) and guess that the third number is 85. Then the average of the three numbers is $\frac{70+85+85}{3} = \frac{240}{3} = 80$. Since this is correct, the answer is choice (C).

Algebraic solution: Note that I strongly recommend that you **do not** use this method on the actual SAT!

If we name the third number x, we have

$$\frac{70 + 85 + x}{3} = 80$$

$$155 + x = 240$$

$$x = 85.$$

So, the answer is choice (C).

Now try to solve each of the following problems by using the strategy you just learned. The answers to these problems, followed by full solutions are at the end of this lesson. **Do not** look at the answers until you have attempted these problems yourself. Please remember to mark off any problems you get wrong.

LEVEL 1: STATISTICS

2. The average (arithmetic mean) of seven numbers is 50. If the sum of six of the numbers is 323, what is the seventh number?

3. For which of the following lists of 5 numbers is the average (arithmetic mean) less than the median?

    (A) 1, 1, 3, 4, 4
    (B) 1, 2, 3, 5, 6
    (C) 1, 1, 3, 5, 5
    (D) 1, 2, 3, 4, 5

LEVEL 2: STATISTICS

4. The average (arithmetic mean) of three numbers is 57. If one of the numbers is 16, what is the sum of the other two?

    (A) 155
    (B) 153
    (C) 107
    (D) 72

5. The average (arithmetic mean) of 22, 50, and y is 50. What is the value of y ?

    (A) 50
    (B) 72
    (C) 76
    (D) 78

6. The average (arithmetic mean) of eight numbers is 260. If a ninth number, 80, is added to the group, what is the average of the nine numbers?

Answers

1. C   4. A
2. 27   5. D
3. A   6. 240

Full Solutions

2.

* Solution by changing averages to sums: We change the average to a sum using the formula

Sum = Average · Number

Here we are averaging 7 numbers. Thus, the **Number** is 7. The **Average** is given to be 50. Therefore, the **Sum** of the 7 numbers is $50 \cdot 7 = 350$. Since we know that the sum of six of the numbers is 323, the seventh number is $350 - 323 = \textbf{27}$.

3.

Solution by changing averages to sums: All of these lists have a median of 3 (this is the number in the middle when the numbers are written in increasing order).

We want the **Average** to be less than 3. So, using the formula

Sum = Average · Number

we see that we want the **Sum** to be less than $3 \cdot 5 = 15$.

Let's start with choice (C). The sum is $1 + 1 + 3 + 5 + 5 = 15$.

Let's try (D) next. $1 + 2 + 3 + 4 + 5 = 15$

Let's try (B). $1 + 2 + 3 + 5 + 6 = 17$

Let's try (A). $1 + 1 + 3 + 4 + 4 = 13$.

Since 13 is less than 15, the answer is choice (A).

* Quick Solution: With a little experience, it is not hard to see that (A) is the answer. Just look at how the numbers are "balanced" about the middle number 3. 1 is two units to the left, and 4 is only 1 unit to the right. You should still compute the sum as a check to verify that the answer is correct.

39

4.

* Solution by changing averages to sums: We are averaging 3 numbers so that the **Number** is 3. The **Average** is given to be 57. Therefore, the **Sum** of the 3 numbers is $57 \cdot 3 = 171$. Since one of the numbers is 16, it follows that the sum of the other two is $171 - 16 = 155$, choice (A).

5.

Solution by changing averages to sums: We are averaging 3 numbers so that the **Number** is 3. The **Average** is given to be 50. Thus, the **Sum** of the 3 numbers is $50 \cdot 3 = 150$. Since we know that two of the numbers are 22 and 50, the third number is $y = 150 - 22 - 50 = 78$, choice (D).

* Quick solution: Since the average is 50, y must be at the same distance from 50 as is it is from 22. The distance between 22 and 50 is $50 - 22 = 28$. It follows that $y = 50 + 28 = 78$, choice (D).

Remark: We can also solve this problem by starting with choice (C).

6.

* Solution by changing averages to sums At first we are averaging eight numbers. Thus, the **Number** is 8. The **Average** is given to be 260. It follows that the **Sum** of the eight numbers is $260 \cdot 8 = 2080$.

When we add 80 to the group the **Sum** becomes $2080 + 80 = 2160$. Thus, the **Average** of the nine numbers is $\frac{2160}{9} = \mathbf{240}$.

OPTIONAL MATERIAL

The following questions will test your understanding of the definitions used in this lesson. These are **not** SAT questions.

Compute the average (arithmetic mean) and median of the following lists of numbers.

1. 1, 2, 3, 4, 5
2. 3, 3, 3, 3, 3
3. 5, 3, 1, -1, -3, -5
4. 21, 57, 32, 48, 1, 101
5. 1, 2, 3, 4, 5,..., 99
6. x, y, z, where $x < y < z$
7. 1, 2, 5, 6, 10, 14, 15, 18, 19

Answers

1. average = median = 3

2. average = median = 3

3. average = median = 0

4. average = $43\frac{1}{3} = \frac{130}{3} \approx 43.3$, median = 40

5. average = median = 50

6. average = $\frac{x+y+z}{3}$, median = y

7. average = median = 10

Tips for Computing These Quickly

You can (and should) compute each of these directly. But in addition, you should try to get the answers quickly using some shortcuts.

1. In a list of consecutive integers, the average (arithmetic mean) and median are equal.

2. If all the numbers in a list are the same, the average and median are equal to that number.

3. **Method 1:** Notice how all of the numbers are "balanced" about 0.

Method 2: Note that the sum is 0 (a quick way to see this is by observing that for each positive number the corresponding negative number is there also).

5. In a list of consecutive integers, the average (arithmetic mean) and median are equal to the average of the first and last number:

$$\frac{1+99}{2} = \frac{100}{2} = 50.$$

7. Notice how all of the numbers are "balanced" about 10 (for example, the distance from 6 to 10 is the same as the distance from 14 to 10).

LESSON 5
HEART OF ALGEBRA

Reminder: Before beginning this lesson remember to redo the problems from Lesson 1 that you have marked off. Do not "unmark" a question unless you get it correct.

When NOT to Start with Choice (B) or (C)

If the word **least** appears in the problem, then start with the smallest number as your first guess. Similarly, if the word **greatest** appears in the problem, then start with the largest number as your first guess.

Try to answer the following question using this strategy. **Do not** check the solution until you have attempted this question yourself.

LEVEL 1: ALGEBRA

1. For which of the following values of k will the value of $7k - 15$ be greater than 6?

(A) 1
(B) 2
(C) 3
(D) 4

* Solution by starting with choice (D): Since the word **greater** appears in the problem let's start with the largest number for our first guess. This is choice (D).

$$7k - 15 = 7 \cdot 4 - 15 = 28 - 15 = 13.$$

Since 13 is greater than 6, the answer is choice (D).

Before we go on, try to solve this problem algebraically (without using the answer choices).

* Algebraic solution:

$$7k - 15 > 6$$
$$7k > 21$$
$$k > 3$$

The only answer choice with a number greater than 3 is choice (D).

Inequalities

$x < y$ means "x is less than y."

For example, $2 < 3$ and $-4 < 0$ are TRUE, whereas $6 < 5$ is FALSE.

$x > y$ means "x is greater than y."

For example, $3 > 2$ and $0 > -4$ are TRUE, whereas $5 > 6$ is FALSE.

It sometimes helps to remember that for $<$ and $>$, the symbol always points to the smaller number.

Before moving on, turn to page 15 and review **Start with choice (B) or (C)**.

Now try to solve each of the following problems by plugging in the answer choices. Then, if possible, solve each problem another way. The answers to these problems, followed by full solutions are at the end of this lesson. **Do not** look at the answers until you have attempted these problems yourself. Please remember to mark off any problems you get wrong.

LEVEL 1: ALGEBRA

2. If $3c + 2 < 11$, which of the following CANNOT be the value of c?

   (A) -1
   (B) 1
   (C) 2
   (D) 3

3. If $z = x - 7$, and $17z - 7z = 30$ what is the value of x?

   (A) 4
   (B) 6
   (C) 8
   (D) 10

43

4. On Thursday, there are the same number of elephants and giraffes at a zoo. The next day 4 of the elephants are released into the wild leaving twice as many giraffes as elephants at the zoo. How many giraffes are at the zoo?

    (A) 4
    (B) 6
    (C) 8
    (D) 12

LEVEL 2: ALGEBRA

5. If $|4 - 7x| > 30$, which of the following is a possible value of x?

    (A) −4
    (B) −2
    (C) 2
    (D) 3

LEVEL 3: ALGEBRA

6. There is the same number of cows, pigs and chickens being transported to a farm. When the transport arrives at the farm, 4 cows are taken off the truck and 8 chickens are placed on the truck. If there are now twice as many pigs as cows on the truck, and twice as many chickens as pigs on the truck, how many chickens are on the truck?

    (A) 6
    (B) 8
    (C) 12
    (D) 16

Answers

1. D	4. C
2. D	5. A
3. D	6. D

44

Full Solutions

2.

Solution by starting with choice (D): Begin by looking at choice (D). We substitute 3 in for c in the given inequality.

$$3c + 2 < 11$$
$$3(3) + 2 < 11$$
$$9 + 2 < 11$$
$$11 < 11$$

Since this is FALSE, the answer is choice (D).

* Remark: This is actually a slight variation of the strategy given in this lesson. A moment's thought should tell you that we are looking for a number that is too big. So, the largest number given must be the answer.

Algebraic solution:

$$3c + 2 < 11$$
$$3c < 9$$
$$c < 3$$

Thus, the answer is choice (D).

3.

Solution by starting with choice (C): We begin by looking at choice (C), and we take a guess that $x = 6$. The first equation gives us $z = x - 7 = 6 - 7 = -1$. It then follows that the left-hand side of the second equation is $17z - 7z = 17(-1) - 7(-1) = -17 + 7 = -10$. This is not equal to 30. The value we chose for x was too small. We can therefore eliminate choices (A), (B), and (C). So, the answer is (D).

Let's just confirm that choice (D) is in fact the answer. We let $x = 10$. Then from the first equation we have that $z = x - 7 = 10 - 7 = 3$. It follows that the left-hand side of the second equation is then $17z - 7z = 17(3) - 7(3) = 51 - 21 = 30$. This is correct so that the answer is choice (D).

* Algebraic solution: We first solve the second equation for z.

$$17z - 7z = 30$$
$$10z = 30$$
$$z = 3$$

45

We now substitute $z = 3$ into the first equation and solve for x.

$$z = x - 7$$
$$3 = x - 7$$

We now add 7 to each side of this equation to get $x = 10$. Therefore, the answer is choice (D).

Remark: Here is the computation in detail referred to in the second to last sentence above.

$$
\begin{array}{r}
3 = x - 7 \\
\underline{+7 \quad\quad +7} \\
10 = x
\end{array}
$$

4.

Solution by starting with choice (C): Let's start with choice (C) and guess that there are 8 giraffes at the zoo. Then there are also 8 elephants at the zoo. After releasing 4 of the elephants into the wild, there are now 4 elephants and 8 giraffes at the zoo. Since there are twice as many giraffes as elephants, this is correct. So, the answer is choice (C).

Algebraic solution: Let x be the number of giraffes at the zoo. After releasing the 4 elephants into the wild, there are x giraffes and $x - 4$ elephants at the zoo. Since there are twice as many giraffes as elephants at the zoo, we have $x = 2(x - 4) = 2x - 8$. So $x = 8$, choice (C).

A detailed look at that last computation: To solve that last equation we subtract x from each side of the equation and then add 8 to each side of the equation. Here are the details.

$$
\begin{array}{r}
x = 2x - 8 \\
\underline{-x \quad\quad -x} \\
0 = \quad x - 8 \\
\underline{+8 \quad\quad\quad +8} \\
8 = \quad x
\end{array}
$$

5.

Solution by starting with choice (C): Let's start with choice (C) and guess that $x = 2$. Then $|4 - 7x| = |4 - 7 \cdot 2| = |4 - 14| = |-10| = 10$. Since 10 is not greater than 30 we can eliminate choice (C).

46

A moment's thought may lead you to suspect choice (A) (if you do not see this it is okay – just keep trying the answer choices until you get to it). Now, setting $x = -4$ gives

$$|4 - 7x| = |4 - 7(-4)| = |4 + 28| = |32| = 32.$$

Since 32 is greater than 30, the answer is choice (A).

* Partial algebraic solution: We can try to simply eliminate the absolute values and solve the resulting inequality.

$$4 - 7x > 30$$
$$-7x > 26$$
$$x < \frac{26}{-7} \approx -3.714$$

Since $-4 < -3.714$, the answer is choice (A).

Note: The inequality changed direction in the last step because we divided each side of the inequality by a negative number.

Complete algebraic solution: The given absolute value inequality is equivalent to $4 - 7x < -30$ or $4 - 7x > 30$. Let's solve these two inequalities simultaneously.

$$4 - 7x < -30 \quad \text{or} \quad 4 - 7x > 30$$
$$-7x < -34 \quad \text{or} \quad -7x > 26$$
$$x > \frac{34}{7} \approx 4.857 \quad \text{or} \quad x < \frac{26}{-7} \approx -3.714$$

So $x < -3.714$ or $x > 4.857$. Since $-4 < -3.714$, the answer is (A).

6.

Solution by starting with choice (B): If there are 8 chickens, then there are 4 pigs, and 2 cows. That means there were originally 0 chickens, 4 pigs, and 6 cows. Since these numbers are not equal we can eliminate choice (B), and choice (A) as well.

Let's try choice (C) next. If there are 12 chickens, then there are 6 pigs, and 3 cows. That means there were originally 4 chickens, 6 pigs, and 7 cows. Again, these numbers are not equal so we can eliminate (C).

Let's verify that the answer is choice (D). If there are 16 chickens, then there are 8 pigs, and 4 cows. That means there were originally 8 of each. So, the answer is choice (D).

* Algebraic solution: Let x be the original number of chickens (so x is also the original number of pigs, and the original number of cows). We then have

$$x = 2(x - 4) \quad \text{and} \quad x + 8 = 2x$$

Each of these equations has the unique solution $x = 8$. So, the number of chickens is

$$x + 8 = 8 + 8 = 16, \text{ choice (D)}.$$

Caution: Before choosing your answer always double check what the question is asking for. In this case, we must find the number of chickens which is $x + 8$, **not** x.

Detailed formal solutions of the above two equations:

$$
\begin{array}{ll}
x = 2(x - 4) & x + 8 = 2x \\
x = 2x - 8 & 8 = x \\
-x = -8 & \\
x = 8 &
\end{array}
$$

Download additional solutions for free here:

www.thesatmathprep.com/28Les400.html

LESSON 6
GEOMETRY

Reminder: Before beginning this lesson remember to redo the problems from Lesson 2 that you have marked off. Do not "unmark" a question unless you get it correct.

Circles and Cylinders

A **circle** is a two-dimensional geometric figure formed of a curved line surrounding a center point, every point of the line being an equal distance from the center point. This distance is called the **radius** of the circle. The **diameter** of a circle is the distance between any two points on the circle that pass through the center of the circle. The perimeter of a circle is called its **circumference** which can be found by using the formula $C = 2\pi r$ where r is the radius of the circle.

Example 1:

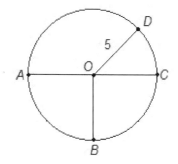

In the figure above we have a circle with center O and radius $r = 5$. Note that $\overline{OA}$, $\overline{OB}$, $\overline{OC}$, and $\overline{OD}$ are all radii of the circle. Also, $\overline{AC}$ is a diameter of the circle with length 10, and the circumference of the circle is $C = 10\pi$.

A **cylinder** is a three-dimensional geometric solid bounded by two equal parallel circles and a curved surface formed by moving a straight line so that its ends lie on the circles. The volume of a cylinder can be found by using the formula $V = \pi r^2 h$ where r is the radius of a base of the cylinder and h is the height of the cylinder.

49

Example 2:

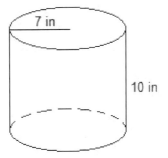

The cylinder above has a base radius of 7 inches and a height of 10 inches. Thus, the volume of the cylinder is $V = \pi(7)^2(10) = 490\pi$ in^3.

Remark: The formulas for the circumference of a circle and the volume of a cylinder are given at the beginning of each math section of the SAT.

Turn to page 42 and review **<u>When not to start with choice (B) or (C)</u>**. Then try to answer the following question using this strategy. **Do not** check the solution until you have attempted this question yourself.

LEVEL 3: GEOMETRY

1. The sum of the areas of two squares is 85. If the sides of both squares have integer lengths, what is the least possible value for the length of a side of the smaller square?

   (A) 1
   (B) 2
   (C) 6
   (D) 7

* Begin by looking at choice (A) since it is the smallest. If the side length of the smaller square is 1, then the area of the smaller square is $1 \cdot 1 = 1$. So the area of the larger square is $85 - 1 = 84$. Since 84 is not a perfect square, we can eliminate choice (A).

Let's try choice (B) next. If the side length of the smaller square is 2, then the area of the smaller square is 4, and the area of the larger square is $85 - 4 = 81$. Since 81 is a perfect square, the answer is choice (B).

Remark: If it is not clear to you that 84 is not a perfect square, take the square root of 84 in your calculator. You will get approximately 9.16515. Since this is not an integer, 84 is not a perfect square.

81 is a perfect square however because $81 = 9^2$. Again, if this is not clear to you, simply take the square root of 81 in your calculator.

Now try to solve each of the following problems. The answers to these problems, followed by full solutions are at the end of this lesson. **Do not** look at the answers until you have attempted these problems yourself. Please remember to mark off any problems you get wrong.

LEVEL 1: GEOMETRY

2.   What is the radius of a circle whose circumference is π?

   (A) $\frac{1}{2}$

   (B) 1

   (C) $\frac{\pi}{2}$

   (D) π

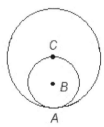

3.   In the figure above, A, B, and C lie on the same line. B is the center of the smaller circle, and C is the center of the larger circle. If the radius of the smaller circle is 7, what is the diameter of the larger circle?

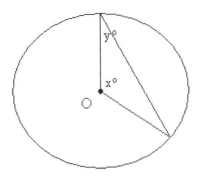

4.   In the figure above, if $y = 32$ and O is the center of the circle, what is the value of x ?

LEVEL 3: GEOMETRY

5.   The volume of a right circular cylinder is 343π cubic centimeters. If the height and base radius of the cylinder are equal, what is the base radius of the cylinder?

   (A) 3 centimeters
   (B) 5 centimeters
   (C) 7 centimeters
   (D) 15 centimeters

Answers

1. B	4. 116
2. A	5. C
3. 28	

Full Solutions

   2.
Solution by starting with choice (C): The circumference of a circle is $C = 2\pi r$. Let's start with choice (C) as our first guess. If $r = \frac{\pi}{2}$, then $C = 2\pi(\frac{\pi}{2}) = \pi^2$. Since this is too big we can eliminate choices (C) and (D).

Let's try choice (B) next. If $r = 1$, then $C = 2\pi(1) = 2\pi$, still too big.

52

The answer must therefore be choice (A). Let's verify this. If $r = \frac{1}{2}$, then $C = 2\pi\left(\frac{1}{2}\right) = \pi$. So, the answer is indeed choice (A).

* Algebraic solution: We use the circumference formula $C = 2\pi r$, and substitute π in for C.

$$C = 2\pi r$$
$$\pi = 2\pi r$$
$$\frac{\pi}{2\pi} = r$$
$$\frac{1}{2} = r$$

This is choice (A).

   3.

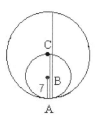

* Since the diameter of a circle is twice the radius, the diameter of the smaller circle is $(2)(7) = 14$. This is also the radius of the larger circle. Therefore, the diameter of the larger circle is $(2)(14) = \mathbf{28}$.

   4.
* Note that the triangle is **isosceles**. In particular, y is equal to the measure of the unlabeled angle. Therefore $x = 180 - 32 - 32 = \mathbf{116}$.

   5.
Solution by starting with choice (C): Let's start with choice (C) as our first guess, so that $r = 7$. Then $h = 7$ too. So, it follows that $V = \pi r^2 h = \pi(7)^2(7) = 343\pi$. This is correct, and so the answer is choice (C).

* Algebraic solution:
$$V = \pi r^2 h$$
$$343\pi = \pi r^2 r$$
$$343 = r^3$$
$$7 = r.$$

Therefore, the answer is choice (C).

OPTIONAL MATERIAL

The following questions will test your understanding of formulas used in this lesson. These are **not** SAT questions.

1. Find the circumference of a circle with each of the following radii.

$$3 \qquad \pi \qquad x \qquad x^2 + 5$$

2. Find the radius of a circle with each of the following circumferences.

$$2\pi \qquad \pi \qquad 7\pi \qquad 5 \qquad C \qquad x - 2$$

3. Find the volume of a cylinder with each of the following base radii and heights.

$$r = h = 2 \qquad r = 3, h = 4 \qquad r = \pi, h = 2\pi \qquad r = x + 1, h = 2x$$

4. Find the height of a cylinder with volume 2π and base radius 5.

5. Find the base radius of a cylinder with volume 100 and height 10.

Answers

1. $6\pi, 2\pi^2, 2\pi x, 2\pi(x^2 + 5)$

2. $1, \dfrac{1}{2}, \dfrac{7}{2}, \dfrac{5}{2\pi}, \dfrac{C}{2\pi}, \dfrac{x-2}{2\pi}$

3. $8\pi, 36\pi, 2\pi^4, \pi(x + 1)^2(2x) = 2\pi x(x + 1)^2$

4. $2\pi = \pi(5)^2 h.$ So $h = \dfrac{2\pi}{\pi(5)^2} = \dfrac{2}{25}$

5. $100 = \pi r^2(10).$ So $r^2 = \dfrac{100}{10\pi} = \dfrac{10}{\pi}.$ So $r = \sqrt{\dfrac{10}{\pi}}$

LESSON 7
PASSPORT TO ADVANCED MATH

Reminder: Before beginning this lesson remember to redo the problems from Lesson 3 that you have marked off. Do not "unmark" a question unless you get it correct.

Graphs of Functions

If f is a function, then

$f(a) = b$ is equivalent to "the point (a, b) lies on the graph of f."

Example 1:

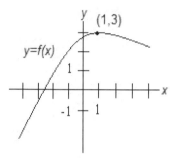

In the figure above we see that the point $(1,3)$ lies on the graph of the function f. Therefore $f(1) = 3$.

Try to answer the following question using this fact. **Do not** check the solution until you have attempted this question yourself.

LEVEL 2: ADVANCED MATH

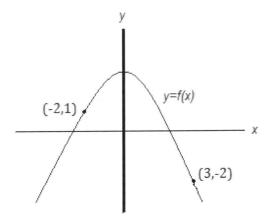

1. The figure above shows the graph of the function f in the xy-plane. What is the value of $f(-2) - f(3)$?

* The points $(-2,1)$ and $(3,-2)$ lie on the graph of the function f. Therefore $f(-2) = 1$ and $f(3) = -2$. So, it follows that $f(-2) - f(3) = 1 - (-2) = 1 + 2 = \mathbf{3}$.

Intercepts

The **y-intercept** of the graph of a function $y = f(x)$ is the point on the graph where $x = 0$ (if it exists). There can be at most one y-intercept for the graph of a function. A y-intercept has the form $(0, b)$ for some real number b. Equivalently, $f(0) = b$.

An **x-intercept** of the graph of a function is a point on the graph where $y = 0$. There can be more than one x-intercept for the graph of a function or none at all. An x-intercept has the form $(a, 0)$ for some real number a. Equivalently, $f(a) = 0$.

Example 2:

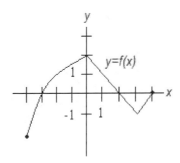

In the figure above we see that the graph of f has y-intercept $(0,2)$ and x-intercepts $(-3,0)$, $(2,0)$ and $(4,0)$.

Equivalently, we have $f(0) = 2$, $f(-3) = 0$, $f(2) = 0$, and $f(4) = 0$.

Now try to answer the following question. **Do not** check the solution until you have attempted this question yourself.

LEVEL 3: ADVANCED MATH

2. The function h is defined by $h(x) = ax + b$, where a and b are constants. In the xy-plane, the graph of $y = h(x)$ crosses the y-axis where $y = 4$ and the x-axis where $x = -2$. What is the value of a ?

* We are given that the point $(0,4)$ is the y-intercept of the graph and $(-2,0)$ is an x-intercept of the graph.

So $h(0) = 4$ and $h(-2) = 0$.

Using the first point gives us $4 = h(0) = a(0) + b$. So $b = 4$ and the function is $h(x) = ax + 4$.

Using the second point gives us $0 = h(-2) = a(-2) + 4 = -2a + 4$. So $2a = 4$, and thus, $a = \dfrac{4}{2} = \mathbf{2}$.

Vertical Line Test

Not every graph is the graph of a function! The graph of a function always passes the **vertical line test**: any vertical line can hit the graph *at most* once.

For example, a circle is *never* the graph of a function. It always fails the vertical line test as shown in the figure below.

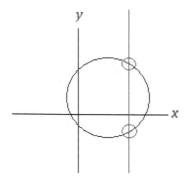

Try to answer the following question using this fact. **Do not** check the solution until you have attempted this question yourself.

LEVEL 1: ADVANCED MATH

3. Which of the following graphs could not be the graph of a function?

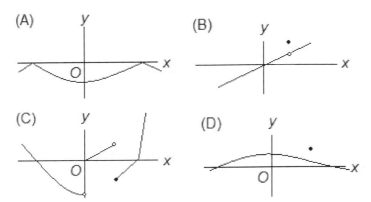

* Only choice (D) fails the **vertical line test**. In other words, we can draw a vertical line that hits the graph more than once:

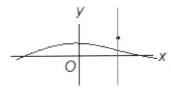

So the answer is choice (D).

Now try to solve each of the following problems. The answers to these problems, followed by full solutions are at the end of this lesson. **Do not** look at the answers until you have attempted these problems yourself. Please remember to mark off any problems you get wrong.

LEVEL 2: ADVANCED MATH

Questions 4 - 5 refer to the following information.

The figure below shows the graph of the function g in the xy-plane.

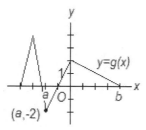

4.   What is the value of $g(b) - g(a)$?

LEVEL 3: ADVANCED MATH

5.   For how many values of x between -4 and 4 does $g(x) = 1$?

6.   In the xy-plane, the graph of the function f, with equation $f(x) = cx^2 - 7$, passes through the point $(-3,38)$. What is the value of c?

Answers

1. 3	4. 2
2. 2	5. 4
3. D	6. 5

Full Solutions

4.
* The points $(a, -2)$ and $(b, 0)$ lie on the graph of the function g. Therefore $g(a) = -2$ and $g(b) = 0$. So $g(b) - g(a) = 0 - (-2) = \mathbf{2}$.

5.
* Let's draw a horizontal line through the point $(0,1)$. To do this find 1 on the y-axis and draw a horizontal line through this point.

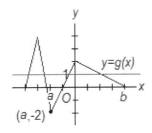

Now observe that this line hits the graph 4 times. So, the answer is **4**.

6.

* Solution: Since the graph of f passes through the point $(-3,38)$, $f(-3) = 38$. But by direct computation

$$f(-3) = c(-3)^2 - 7 = 9c - 7.$$

So $9c - 7 = 38$. Therefore $9c = 38 + 7 = 45$, and so $c = \dfrac{45}{9} = $ **5**.

Download additional solutions for free here:

www.thesatmathprep.com/28Les400.html

LESSON 8
PROBLEM SOLVING

Reminder: Before beginning this lesson remember to redo the problems from Lesson 4 that you have marked off. Do not "unmark" a question unless you get it correct.

Simple Probability Principle

To compute a simple probability where all outcomes are equally likely, divide the number of "successes" by the total number of outcomes.

Try to answer the following question using the simple probability principle. **Do not** check the solution until you have attempted this question yourself.

LEVEL 1: PROBLEM SOLVING

3, 5, 6, 15, 27, 35, 45, 75

1. A number is to be selected at random from the list above. What is the probability that the number selected will be less than 30 ?

* The total number of outcomes is 8. The number of "successes" is 5. Therefore, the probability is **5/8 or .625**.

Note: In this problem, a "success" is a number that is less than 30.

The "successes" are 3, 5, 6, 15, and 27.

Conditional Probability

A **conditional probability** measures the probability of an event given that another event has occurred. Let's use an example to illustrate conditional probability.

LEVEL 2: PROBLEM SOLVING

Questions 2 - 3 refer to the following information.

A survey was conducted among a randomly chosen sample of 100 males and 100 females to gather data on pet ownership. The data are shown in the table below.

	Has pets	Does not have pets	Total
Men	75	25	100
Women	63	37	100
Total	138	62	200

2. According to the table, what is the probability that a randomly selected man does not have pets?

* There are a total of 100 men, and of these men 25 do not have pets. So, the desired probability is $\frac{25}{100} = $ **1/4 or .25**.

Notes: (1) The denominator of the fraction is 100, the total number of men. To find this number we look in the column labeled "Total" and the row labeled "Men."

(2) The numerator of the fraction is 25, the number of men who do not have pets. To find this number we look in the column labeled "Does not have pets" and the row labeled "Men."

3. * According to the table, what is the probability that a randomly selected person with pets is female?

62

* There are 138 people who have pets, and of these 63 are women. So, the desired probability is $\frac{63}{138} \approx .4565217$. So, we can grid in **.456** or **.457**.

Now try to solve each of the following problems. The answers to these problems, followed by full solutions are at the end of this lesson. **Do not** look at the answers until you have attempted these problems yourself. Please remember to mark off any problems you get wrong.

LEVEL 3: PROBLEM SOLVING

Questions 4 - 7 refer to the following information.

The data in the table below categorizes the GPAs of the students from two high schools.

	Less than 2.5	Between 2.5 and 3.5	Greater than 3.5	Total
School A	272	117	36	425
School B	146	308	121	575
Total	358	425	217	1000

4. * If a student with a GPA between 2.5 and 3.5 is chosen at random, what is the probability that the student goes to school B?

5. * What is the probability that a randomly selected student is from school A with a GPA greater than 3.5?

6. * If a student from School A is chosen at random, what is the probability that the student has a GPA of at least 2.5?

Answers

1. 5/8 or .625   4. .724 or .725
2. 1/4 or .25   5. .036
3. .456 or .457   6. 9/25 or .36

Full Solutions

4.

* This is a conditional probability. We want the probability the student goes to school B *given* the student has a GPA between 2.5 and 3.5. This is $\frac{308}{425} \approx .724$ or $.725$.

5.

* There are 36 students from school A with a GPA greater than 3.5, and there is a total of 1000 students. So, the desired probability is $\frac{36}{1000} = .036$.

Note: This is not a conditional probability.

6.

* This is a conditional probability. We want the probability the student has a GPA of at least 2.5 *given* the student is from school A. Note that a student has a GPA of at least 2.5 if the student has a GPA between 2.5 and 3.5 **or** the student has a GPA greater than 3.5. So, the desired probability is $\frac{117+36}{425} = 9/25$ or $.36$.

Download additional solutions for free here:

www.thesatmathprep.com/28Les400.html

LESSON 9
ALGEBRA

Reminder: Before beginning this lesson remember to redo the problems from Lessons 1 and 5 that you have marked off. Do not "unmark" a question unless you get it correct.

Take a Guess

Sometimes the answer choices themselves cannot be substituted in for the unknown or unknowns in the problem. But that doesn't mean you can't guess your own numbers. Try to make as reasonable a guess as possible, but don't over think it. Keep trying until you zero in on the correct value.

Try to answer the following question using this strategy. **Do not** check the solution until you have attempted this question yourself.

LEVEL 1: ALGEBRA

1. If $4x - 12 = 8$, then $42 - 3x =$

* Solution by taking a guess: Let's start with a "random" guess for x, let's say $x = 6$. So, let's plug 6 in for x in the first equation.

$$4x - 12 = 8$$
$$4 \cdot 6 - 12 = 8$$
$$24 - 12 = 8$$
$$12 = 8$$

Our guess was too big. So, let's take a smaller guess like 5.

$$4x - 12 = 8$$
$$4 \cdot 5 - 12 = 8$$
$$20 - 12 = 8$$
$$8 = 8$$

It worked. So $x = 5$. Thus, $42 - 3x = 42 - 3 \cdot 5 = 42 - 15 = \textbf{27}$.

65

Before we go on, try to solve this problem algebraically.

* Algebraic solution: We solve the first equation for x by adding 12 to each side of the equation. We get $4x = 20$. We divide each side of this equation by 4 to get $x = 5$. So $42 - 3x = 42 - 3 \cdot 5 = 42 - 15 = \mathbf{27}$.

Now try to solve each of the following problems. Whenever possible, use the strategy of taking a guess. Then, if possible, solve each problem another way. The answers to these problems, followed by full solutions are at the end of this lesson. **Do not** look at the answers until you have attempted these problems yourself. Please remember to mark off any problems you get wrong.

LEVEL 1: ALGEBRA

2. If $3y - 18 = 15$, then $y - 6 =$

    (A) 5
    (B) 10
    (C) 15
    (D) 20

3. If $k > 0$, for what value of k will $k^2 - 4 = 21$?

LEVEL 2: ALGEBRA

4. If $3x + 7 = 24$, then $3x - 7 =$

    (A) 8
    (B) 9
    (C) 10
    (D) 11

$$\sqrt{10b^2 - 9} + x = 0$$

5. If $b > 0$ and $x = -9$ in the equation above, what is the value of b?

LEVEL 3: ALGEBRA

6. If $3^x = 11$, then $3^{2x} =$

    (A) 5.5
    (B) 22
    (C) 33
    (D) 121

Answers

1. 27   4. C
2. A   5. 3
3. 5   6. D

Full Solutions

2.

Solution by taking a guess: Let's start with a "random" guess for y, say $y = 10$. So let's plug 10 in for y in the first equation.

$$3y - 18 = 15$$
$$3 \cdot 10 - 18 = 15$$
$$30 - 18 = 15$$
$$12 = 15$$

It looks as though 10 is a little too small. $y = 11$ should do the trick.

$$3y - 18 = 15$$
$$3 \cdot 11 - 18 = 15$$
$$33 - 18 = 15$$
$$15 = 15$$

So y is, in fact, 11. Thus, $y - 6 = 11 - 6 = 5$, and the answer is (A).

Algebraic solution: We solve for y algebraically.

$$3y - 18 = 15$$
$$3y = 33$$
$$y = 11$$

So $y - 6 = 11 - 6 = 5$, and the answer is choice (A).

* Quicker algebraic solution: We solve for $y - 6$ algebraically.

$$3y - 18 = 15$$
$$3(y - 6) = 15$$
$$y - 6 = 5$$

Thus, the answer is choice (A).

3.

* Solution by taking a guess: Let's take a guess for k, say $k = 5$. Then $k^2 - 4 = 5^2 - 4 = 25 - 4 = 21$. This is correct. So, the answer is **5**.

Algebraic solution:

$$k^2 - 4 = 21$$
$$k^2 = 25$$
$$k = 5$$

Remark: The equation $k^2 = 25$ has two solutions: $k = 5$ and $k = -5$. In this question, we are given that $k > 0$, so we reject the negative solution. In easy problems (Level 1 and Level 2), it is pretty safe to reject the negative solution (or not even think about it), but in medium and hard problems (Levels 3, 4 and 5) you may need to be more careful.

* Mental math: $25 - 4 = 21$. So $k = 5$.

Remark: For more information on this technique see the discussion on informal algebra in Lesson 1.

4.

Solution by taking a guess: Let's start with a "random" guess for x, let's say $x = 5$. So, let's plug 5 in for x in the given equation.

$$3x + 7 = 24$$
$$3 \cdot 5 + 7 = 24$$
$$15 + 7 = 24$$
$$22 = 24$$

This guess was just a bit too small. Let's try 6.

$$3x + 7 = 24$$
$$3 \cdot 6 + 7 = 24$$
$$18 + 7 = 24$$
$$25 = 24$$

Oh no – it looks like the answer is a number between 5 and 6. Let's substitute both 5 and 6 into the given expression.

$$3 \cdot 5 - 7 = 15 - 7 = 8$$
$$3 \cdot 6 - 7 = 18 - 7 = 11$$

So, the answer is a number between 8 and 11, thus narrowing our choices down to (B) and (C). Since attempting 6 came out closer to correct, (C) seems like the better choice. The answer is, in fact, choice (C).

Algebraic solution: An algebraic solution is a much better choice in this example.

$$3x + 7 = 24$$
$$3x = 17$$
$$3x - 7 = 10$$

Thus, the answer is choice (C).

Remark: Note that we did not need to get x by itself, since $3x$ appeared in both the equation and the expression. We can think of $3x$ as a **block**. For more information on blocks see Lesson 17.

* Quicker algebraic solution: We can actually do the algebra in a single step by subtracting 14 from each side of the equation.

$$3x + 7 = 24$$
$$3x - 7 = 10$$

Thus, the answer is choice (C).

5.

Solution by taking a guess: When we replace x by -9 we get

$$\sqrt{10b^2 - 9} - 9 = 0.$$

Let's start with a "random" guess for b, let's say $b = 5$. So, let's plug 5 in for b in the equation above.

$$\sqrt{10(5)^2 - 9} - 9 = \sqrt{10 \cdot 25 - 9} - 9 = \sqrt{250 - 9} - 9 = \sqrt{241} - 9.$$

Since $\sqrt{241} > 9$, our guess was too big.

Let's try $b = 3$ next. We then have the following.

$$\sqrt{10(3)^2 - 9} - 9 = \sqrt{90 - 9} - 9 = \sqrt{81} - 9 = 9 - 9 = 0.$$

So, the answer is **3**.

Algebraic solution: As in the previous solution we replace x by -9 to get

$$\sqrt{10b^2 - 9} - 9 = 0, \text{ or equivalently, } \sqrt{10b^2 - 9} = 9$$

We square each side of this last equation to get $10b^2 - 9 = 81$.

We then add 9 to get $10b^2 = 90$, and divide by 10 to get $b^2 = 9$. Since $3^2 = 9$, the answer is **3**.

Remark: To solve the equation $b^2 = 9$ formally requires the **square root property**. There are two solutions to this equation: $b = 3$ and $b = -3$. See Lesson 23 for more on the square root property.

6.

Solution by taking a guess: Let's try to guess what x is. $3^2 = 9$, and $3^3 = 27$. So x is between 2 and 3. Now, $3^{2.2} = 3^4 = 81$ and $3^{2.3} = 3^6 = 729$. Therefore, the answer is between 81 and 729. Thus, the answer must be choice (D).

* **Algebraic solution:** $3^{2x} = (3^x)^2 = 11^2 = 121$. Thus, the answer is choice (D).

See the optional material below for a review of the basic laws of exponents.

OPTIONAL MATERIAL

Basic Laws of Exponents

Here is a brief review of the basic laws of exponents.

Law	Example
$x^0 = 1$	$3^0 = 1$
$x^1 = x$	$9^1 = 9$
$x^a x^b = x^{a+b}$	$x^3 x^5 = x^8$
$x^a / x^b = x^{a-b}$	$x^{11} / x^4 = x^7$
$(x^a)^b = x^{ab}$	$(x^5)^3 = x^{15}$
$(xy)^a = x^a y^a$	$(xy)^4 = x^4 y^4$
$(x/y)^a = x^a / y^a$	$(x/y)^6 = x^6 / y^6$

Now let's practice. Simplify the following expressions using the basic laws of exponents.

1. $5^2 \cdot 5^3$

2. $\dfrac{5^3}{5^2}$

3. $\dfrac{x^5 \cdot x^3}{x^8}$

4. $(2^3)^4$

5. $\dfrac{(xy)^7 (yz)^2}{y^9}$

6. $\left(\dfrac{2}{3}\right)^3 \left(\dfrac{9}{4}\right)^2$

7. $\dfrac{x^4 + x^2}{x^2}$

8. $\dfrac{(x^{10} + x^9 + x^8)(y^5 + y^4)}{y^4(x^2 + x + 1)}$

Answers

1. $5^5 = 3125$

2. $5^1 = 5$

3. $\dfrac{x^8}{x^8} = 1$

4. $2^{12} = 4096$

5. $\dfrac{x^7 y^7 y^2 z^2}{y^9} = \dfrac{x^7 y^9 z^2}{y^9} = x^7 z^2$

6. $\dfrac{2^3}{3^3} \cdot \dfrac{9^2}{4^2} = \dfrac{2^3}{3^3} \cdot \dfrac{(3^2)^2}{(2^2)^2} = \dfrac{2^3}{3^3} \cdot \dfrac{3^4}{2^4} = \dfrac{3^1}{2^1} = \dfrac{3}{2}$

7. $\dfrac{x^2(x^2 + 1)}{x^2} = x^2 + 1$

8. $\dfrac{x^8(x^2 + x + 1)y^4(y + 1)}{y^4(x^2 + x + 1)} = x^8(y + 1)$

71

LESSON 10
GEOMETRY

Reminder: Before beginning this lesson remember to redo the problems from Lessons 2 and 6 that you have marked off. Do not "unmark" a question unless you get it correct.

Figures are Drawn to Scale Unless Otherwise Stated

Try to answer the following question using this strategy. **Do not** check the solution until you have attempted this question yourself.

LEVEL 1: GEOMETRY

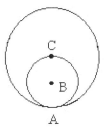

1. In the figure above, $A, B,$ and C lie on the same line. B is the center of the smaller circle, and C is the center of the larger circle. If the radius of the smaller circle is 6, what is the diameter of the larger circle?

* Solution by assuming the figure is drawn to scale: We can assume that the figure is drawn to scale.

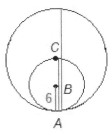

The three lines drawn in the picture above are just there for the purposes of measurement. In practice, you can just use your fingers to measure.

72

The smallest segment is the radius of the smaller circle. The longest segment is the diameter of the larger circle.

From the picture, it is easy to see that the diameter of the larger circle is 4 times the radius of the smaller circle. So, the answer is $(4)(6) = $ **24**.

Before we go on, try to give a complete geometric solution.

* Geometric solution: Since the diameter of a circle is twice the radius, the diameter of the smaller circle is $(2)(6) = 12$. This is also the radius of the larger circle. Therefore, the diameter of the larger circle is $(2)(12) = $ **24**.

Draw Your Own Figure

Try to answer the following question using this strategy. **Do not** check the solution until you have attempted this question yourself.

LEVEL 2: GEOMETRY

2.   In the xy-plane, the point $(0,2)$ is the center of a circle that has radius 2. Which of the following is NOT a point on the circle?

   (A) $(0, 4)$
   (B) $(-2, 4)$
   (C) $(2, 2)$
   (D) $(-2, 2)$

* Solution by drawing a picture:

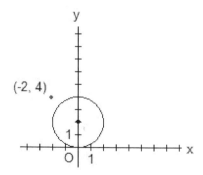

From the picture, it should be clear that $(-2, 4)$ is not on the circle. This is choice (B).

73

Turn to page 65 and review **Take a Guess**. Then try to answer the following question using this strategy. **Do not** check the solution until you have attempted this question yourself.

LEVEL 1: GEOMETRY

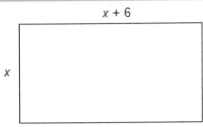

3.   If the area of the rectangle above is 55, what is the value of x?

* **Solution by taking a guess:** Recall that we get the **area** of a rectangle by multiplying the length and the width of the rectangle. Let's start with $x = 10$ as our first guess. Then $x + 6 = 10 + 6 = 16$. So, the area is $10(16) = 160$. This is too big. So, let's try $x = 5$. Then we have $x + 6 = 5 + 6 = 11$. So, the area is $5(11) = 55$. This is correct so that the answer is **5**.

Before we go on, try to solve this problem algebraically.

Algebraic solution:
$$A = lw$$
$$55 = x(x + 6)$$
$$55 = x^2 + 6x$$
$$x^2 + 6x - 55 = 0$$
$$(x + 11)(x - 5) = 0$$
$$x + 11 = 0 \ \text{ or } \ x - 5 = 0$$
$$x = -11 \ \text{ or } \ x = 5$$

So, the answer is **5**.

Note: We reject -11 because a length cannot be negative. Also, you can never grid in a negative number.

Now try to solve each of the following problems using one of the three strategies we just went over. Then, if possible, solve each problem another way. The answers to these problems, followed by full solutions are at the end of this lesson. **Do not** look at the answers until you have attempted these problems yourself. Please remember to mark off any problems you get wrong.

LEVEL 3: GEOMETRY

4. The volume of a right circular cylinder is 1024π cubic centimeters. If the height is twice the base radius of the cylinder, what is the base radius of the cylinder?

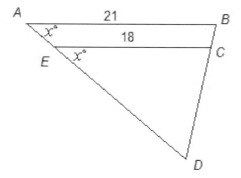

5. In the figure above, what is the value of $\frac{ED}{AD}$?

(A) $\frac{1}{7}$

(B) $\frac{2}{5}$

(C) $\frac{1}{2}$

(D) $\frac{6}{7}$

LEVEL 4: GEOMETRY

6. Point A is a vertex of a 6-sided polygon. The polygon has 6 sides of equal length and 6 angles of equal measure. When all possible diagonals are drawn from point A in the polygon, how many triangles are formed?

   (A) One
   (B) Two
   (C) Three
   (D) Four

Answers

1. 24	4. 8
2. B	5. D
3. 5	6. D

Full Solutions

4.

Solution by taking a guess: Let's start with a guess of $r = 6$. Then $h = 12$, so that $V = \pi r^2 h = \pi(6)^2(12) = 432\pi$, too small. Let's try $r = 8$ next. Then $h = 16$, and so $V = \pi r^2 h = \pi(8)^2(16) = 1024\pi$. This is correct, and so the base radius is **8**.

* Algebraic solution:

$$V = \pi r^2 h$$
$$1024\pi = \pi r^2(2r)$$
$$512 = r^3$$
$$8 = r.$$

Therefore, the answer is **8**.

5.

* Solution by assuming the figure is drawn to scale: Clearly ED is more than half the size of AD, so that $\frac{ED}{AD} > \frac{1}{2}$. Thus, the answer is $\frac{6}{7}$, choice (D).

6.

* **Solution by drawing your own figure:** We draw a picture.

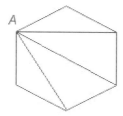

Observe that there are four triangles, choice (D).

OPTIONAL MATERIAL

The following questions will test your understanding of some basic formulas. These are **not** SAT questions.

1.   Find the perimeter of a square with area 49.

2.   Find the area of a square with perimeter 48.

3.   Find the area of a rectangle with perimeter of 100 and length 20.

4.   Find the perimeter of a rectangle with area 35 and width 7.

5.   Find the area of a rectangle with perimeter 100.

Answers

1. $4(7) = 28$

2. $(\frac{48}{4})^2 = 12^2 = 144$

3. $w = \frac{100 - 2(20)}{2} = \frac{100 - 40}{2} = \frac{60}{2} = 30$. So $A = (20)(30) = 600$

4. $\ell = \frac{35}{7} = 5$. So $P = 2(5) + 2(7) = 10 + 14 = 24$.

5. **Cannot be determined from the given information!** For example, in question 4 we saw that A can be 600. But, for example, if $\ell = 10$, then $w = \frac{100 - 2(10)}{2} = \frac{100 - 20}{2} = \frac{80}{2} = 40$. So $A = (10)(40) = 400$.

LESSON 11
PASSPORT TO ADVANCED MATH

Reminder: Before beginning this lesson remember to redo the problems from Lessons 3 and 7 that you have marked off. Do not "unmark" a question unless you get it correct.

Functions and Their Graphs

I suggest that you carefully review lesson 3 and 7 before beginning this lesson.

Fact: If the graph of $f(x)$ is above the x-axis, then $f(x) > 0$. If the graph of f is below the x-axis, then $f(x) < 0$. If the graph of f is higher than the graph of g, then $f(x) > g(x)$.

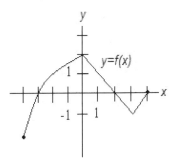

Example 1: In the figure above, observe that $f(x) < 0$ for $-4 \leq x < -3$ and $2 < x < 4$. Also, observe that $f(x) > 0$ for $-3 < x < 2$.

Try to answer the following question using the above fact. **Do not** check the solution until you have attempted this question yourself.

LEVEL 2: ADVANCED MATH

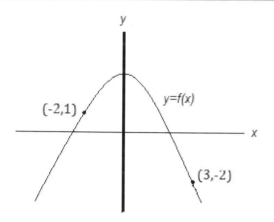

1. The figure above shows the graph of the function f in the xy-plane. For which of the following values of x is $f(x) < 0$?

   (A) -2
   (B) $\ 0$
   (C) $\ 1$
   (D) $\ 3$

* When $x = 3$, the graph of f is below the x-axis. So $f(3) < 0$ and the answer is choice (D).

Points of Intersection

A point (x, y) is a solution of a system of equations if the point is on the graph of *all* equations in the system.

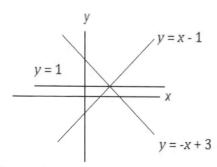

Example 2: The figure above shows three graphs in the xy-plane. These are the graphs of the following system of equations:

$$y = x - 1$$
$$y = -x + 3$$
$$y = 1$$

Form the graphs we see that this system has one solution. It is the point of intersection of all 3 graphs.

To find this point observe that all three points must have y-coordinate 1 (because $y = 1$ is one of the equations). We can now substitute $y = 1$ into either of the other two equations to find x. For example, $1 = x - 1$ implies that $x = 2$. So, the only solution to the given system is $(2, 1)$.

Now try to answer the following question. **Do not** check the solution until you have attempted this question yourself.

LEVEL 1: ADVANCED MATH

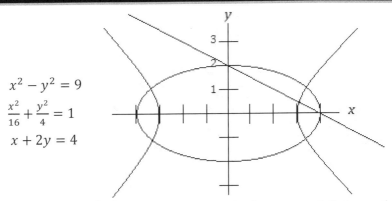

$$x^2 - y^2 = 9$$
$$\frac{x^2}{16} + \frac{y^2}{4} = 1$$
$$x + 2y = 4$$

2. A system of three equations in two unknowns and their graphs in the xy-plane are shown above. How many solutions does the system have?

* Solution by looking at the graph: There is no point that is common to all three graphs. So, the system has no solutions. The answer is **0**.

Notes: (1) A solution to the system of equations is a point that satisfies all three equations simultaneously. Graphically this means that the point is on all three graphs. Although there are several points that are common to two of the graphs, there are none that are common to all three.

(2) The graph of the equation $x^2 - y^2 = 9$ is the **hyperbola** in the figure above with **vertices** $(-3,0)$ and $(3,0)$.

80

(3) The graph of the equation $\frac{x^2}{16} + \frac{y^2}{4} = 1$ is the **ellipse** in the figure above with vertices $(-4,0)$, $(4,0)$, $(0,2)$, and $(0,-2)$

(4) The graph of the equation $x + 2y = 4$ is the **line** in the figure above with **intercepts** $(4,0)$ and $(0,2)$.

$(4,0)$ is the **x-intercept** of the line, and $(0,2)$ is the **y-intercept** of the line.

(5) Consider the following system of equations:

$$\frac{x^2}{16} + \frac{y^2}{4} = 1$$
$$x + 2y = 4$$

This system has the two solutions $(0,2)$ and $(4,0)$. These are the two points common to the graphs of these two equations (the ellipse and the line), also known as **points of intersection** of the two graphs.

(6) Consider the following system of equations:

$$x^2 - y^2 = 9$$
$$x + 2y = 4$$

This system also has two solutions. These are the two points common to the hyperbola and the line. Finding these two solutions requires solving the system algebraically, which we won't do here.

One of these solutions can be seen on the graph. It looks to be approximately $(3.1, 0.5)$.

The second solution does not appear on the portion of the graph that is displayed. If we continued to graph the line and hyperbola to the left, we would see them intersect one more time.

(6) Consider the following system of equations:

$$x^2 - y^2 = 9$$
$$\frac{x^2}{16} + \frac{y^2}{4} = 1$$

This system has four solutions. These are the four points common to the hyperbola and the ellipse. Finding these four solutions requires solving the system algebraically, which we won't do here. These solutions can be seen clearly on the graph.

Now try to solve each of the following problems. The answers to these problems, followed by full solutions are at the end of this lesson. **Do not** look at the answers until you have attempted these problems yourself. Please remember to mark off any problems you get wrong.

LEVEL 2: ADVANCED MATH

$$k(x) = \frac{3}{7}x + c$$

3. In the function above, c is a constant. If $k(14) = 11$, what is the value of $k(-7)$?

LEVEL 3: ADVANCED MATH

4. The function h is defined by $h(x) = 5x^2 - cx + 3$, where c is a constant. In the xy-plane, the graph of $y = h(x)$ crosses the x-axis where $x = 1$. What is the value of c ?

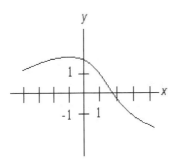

5. The figure above shows the graph of the function f. Which of the following is less than $f(1)$?

(A) $f(-3)$
(B) $f(-2)$
(C) $f(0)$
(D) $f(3)$

82

LEVEL 4: ADVANCED MATH

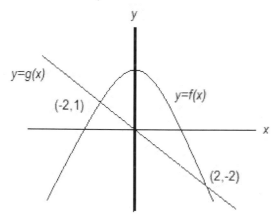

6. In the xy-plane above, the graph of the function f is a parabola, and the graph of the function g is a line. The graphs of f and g intersect at $(-2,1)$ and $(2,-2)$. For which of the following values of x is $f(x) - g(x) < 0$?

(A) -3
(B) -1
(C) $\ \ 0$
(D) $\ \ 1$

Answers

1. D	4. 8
2. 0	5. D
3. 2	6. A

Full Solutions

3.

* $k(14) = \frac{3}{7}(14) + c = 6 + c$. Since we are given that $k(14) = 11$, we have $6 + c = 11$, and so $c = 11 - 6 = 5$.

So $k(x) = \frac{3}{7}x + 5$, and therefore $k(-7) = \frac{3}{7}(-7) + 5 = -3 + 5 = \mathbf{2}$.

4.

* A graph crosses the x-axis at a point where $y = 0$. Thus, the point $(1, 0)$ is on the graph of $y = h(x)$. So,

$$0 = h(1) = 5(1)^2 - c + 3 = 5 - c + 3 = 8 - c.$$

So $8 - c = 0$, and therefore $c = \mathbf{8}$.

5.

* Let's draw a horizontal line through the point $(1, f(1))$. To do this start on the x-axis at 1 and go straight up until you hit the curve. This height is $f(1)$. Now draw a horizontal line through this point.

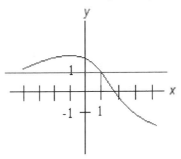

Now, notice that the graph is below this line when $x = 3$. So $f(3)$ is less than $f(1)$. Therefore, the answer is choice (D).

6.

Solution by starting with choice (C): Let's add some information to the picture.

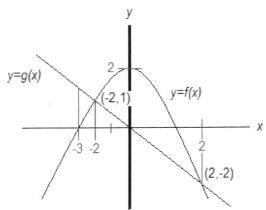

84

Now let's start with choice (C). Since the point $(0,2)$ is on the graph of f, we have that $f(0) = 2$. Since the point $(0,0)$ is on the graph of g, we have $g(0) = 0$. So $f(0) - g(0) = 2 - 0 = 2 > 0$. So, we can eliminate choice (C).

A moment's thought should lead you to suspect that choice (A) might be the answer (if you do not see this it is okay – just keep trying answer choices until you get there). Since the point $(-3,0)$ is on the graph of f, we have $f(-3) = 0$. It looks like $(-3,1.5)$ is on the graph of g, so that $g(-3) = 1.5$. So $f(-3) - g(-3) = 0 - 1.5 = -1.5 < 0$. Thus, the answer is choice (A).

* Geometric solution: $f(x) - g(x) < 0$ is equivalent to $f(x) < g(x)$. Graphically this means that $f(x)$ is lower than $g(x)$. This happens at $x = -3$, choice (A).

Remark: If $-2 < x < 2$, then the graph of f is higher than the graph of g. This means that $f(x) > g(x)$, or equivalently $f(x) - g(x) > 0$. If $x < -2$ or $x > 2$, then the graph of f is lower than the graph of g. This means $f(x) < g(x)$, or equivalently $f(x) - g(x) < 0$.

Download additional solutions for free here:

www.thesatmathprep.com/28Les400.html

LESSON 12
DATA ANALYSIS

Reminder: Before beginning this lesson remember to redo the problems from Lessons 4 and 8 that you have marked off. Do not "unmark" a question unless you get it correct.

Scatterplots

A scatterplot is a graph of plotted points that show the relationship between two sets of data. On the SAT the "line of best fit" is sometimes drawn over a given scatterplot.

Example 1: Take a look at the following scatterplot.

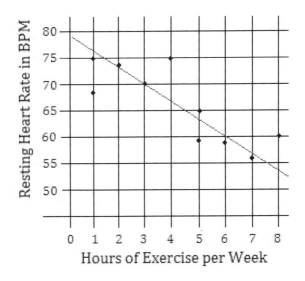

There are 10 data points in this scatterplot. Each point represents a person. The x-coordinate of the point tells us how many hours that person exercises per week, and the y-coordinate of the point tells us the resting heart rate of that person. For example, there is a person that exercises 1 hour per week with a resting heart rate of 75 BPM (beats per minute), and there is also another person that exercises 1 hour per week with a resting heart rate of approximately 68 BPM

The line that is drawn in the figure is the line of best fit. It is the line that gives the best overall approximation of all the data points.

86

Scatterplot Classification

The following scatterplots show **positive associations**.

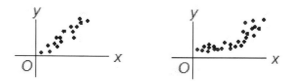

The scatterplot on the left shows a linear positive association, whereas the scatterplot on the right shows a nonlinear positive association. The rightmost scatterplot looks like it might show an exponential positive association.

Here are a few more scatterplots.

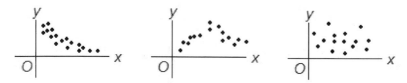

The leftmost scatterplot shows a nonlinear (possibly exponential) **negative association**, whereas the other two show **no association**.

Other Graph Types

Several other types of graphs may appear on the SAT such as bar graphs, line graphs, circle graphs, and histograms. Here is an example of an SAT math problem involving a line graph.

LEVEL 2: DATA ANALYSIS

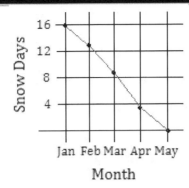

1. The line graph above shows the average number of days that it snows at least 0.1 inch in Buffalo, NY from January to May. According to the graph, approximately what was the greatest decrease in the number of snow days from one month to the next month?

   (A) 2
   (B) 3
   (C) 4
   (D) 6

* The greatest decrease occurs from March to April. It is approximately $9 - 3 = 6$, choice (D).

Note: The decrease from Jan to Feb is approximately $16 - 13 = 3$.

The decrease from Feb to Mar is approximately $13 - 9 = 4$.

The decrease from Mar to Apr is approximately $9 - 3 = 6$.

The decrease from Apr to May is approximately $3 - 0 = 3$.

Now try to solve each of the following problems. The answers to these problems, followed by full solutions are at the end of this lesson. **Do not** look at the answers until you have attempted these problems yourself. Please remember to mark off any problems you get wrong.

LEVEL 1: DATA ANALYSIS

Questions 2 - 5 refer to the following information.

Ten 25-year-old men were asked how many hours per week they exercise and their resting heart rate was taken in beats per minute (BPM). The results are shown as points in the scatterplot below, and the line of best fit is drawn.

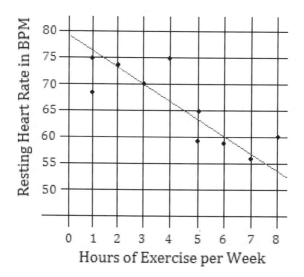

2. How many of the men have a resting heart rate that differs by more than 5 BPM from the resting heart rate predicted by the line of best fit?

    (A) None
    (B) Two
    (C) Three
    (D) Four

3. Based on the line of best fit, what is the predicted resting heart rate for someone that exercises three and a half hours per week?

    (A) 66 BPM
    (B) 68 BPM
    (C) 70 BPM
    (D) 72 BPM

4. What is the resting heart rate, in BPM, of the man represented by the data point that is farthest from the line of best fit?

    (A) 60
    (B) 66
    (C) 68
    (D) 75

5. Which of the following is the best interpretation of the slope of the line of best fit in the context of this problem?

    (A) The predicted number of hours that a person must exercise to maintain a resting heart rate of 50 BPM.
    (B) The predicted resting heart rate of a person that does not exercise.
    (C) The predicted decrease in resting heart rate, in BPM, for each one-hour increase in weekly exercise.
    (D) The predicted increase in the number of hours of exercise needed to increase the resting heart rate by one BPM.

LEVEL 3: DATA ANALYSIS

6. Which of the following graphs best shows a strong negative association between x and y ?

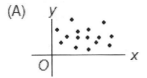

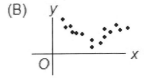

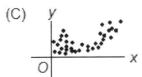

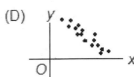

7. According to the line graph above, the mean annual salary of an NBA player in 1981 was what fraction of the mean annual salary of an NBA player in 1984 ?

LEVEL 4: DATA ANALYSIS

SURVEY RESULTS

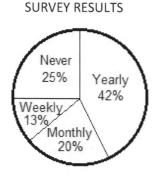

8. The circle graph above shows the distribution of responses to a survey in which a group of people were asked how often they donate to charity. What fraction of those surveyed reported that they donate at least yearly?

Answers

1. D   5. C
2. C   6. D
3. B   7. 4/7 or .571
4. C   8. 3/4 or .75

Full Solutions

2.

* The points that are more than 5 BPM away from the line of best fit occur at 1, 4, and 8 hours. So, there are Three of them, choice (C).

Notes: (1) One of the two men that exercise 1 hour per week has a resting heart rate of approximately 68 BPM. The line of best fit predicts approximately 77 BPM. So, this difference is $77 - 68 = 9$ BPM.

Similarly, at 4 we have a difference of approximately $75 - 67 = 8$ BPM, and at 8 we have a difference of approximately $60 - 54 = 6$ BPM.

(2) At 5, the point below the curve corresponds to a heart rate that differs from that predicted by the line of best fit by approximately $64 - 59 = 5$ BPM. Since this is not *more than* 5, we do not include this point in the count.

3.

* The point $(3.5, 68)$ seems to be on the line of best fit. So, the answer is 68 BPM, choice (B).

4.

* The data point that is furthest from the line of best fit is at $(1,68)$. This point represents a man with a resting heart rate of 68 BPM, choice (C).

5.

* The slope of the line is $\frac{\text{change in predicted heart rate}}{\text{change in hours of exercise}}$. If we make the denominator a 1-hour increase, then the fraction is the change in predicted heart rate per 1-hour increase. Since the line is moving downward from left to right, we can replace "change" in the numerator by "decrease." So, the answer is choice (C).

*Note: Recall that the slope of a line is

$$\text{Slope} = m = \frac{\text{rise}}{\text{run}} = \frac{\text{change in vertical distance}}{\text{change in horizontal distance}}$$

In this problem, the change in vertical distance is the change in resting heart rate, in BPM, and the change in horizontal distance is the change in hours of exercise per week.

6.

* Only the scatterplot in choice (D) is continually moving downward from left to right. So, the answer is choice (D).

7.

* According to the graph the mean annual salary of an NBA player in 1981 was \$200,000 and the mean annual salary of an NBA player in 1984 was \$350,000. So, the answer is $\frac{200,000}{350,000} = $ **4/7** or **.571**.

8.

* "At least yearly" means yearly, monthly, or weekly. So, the answer is $\frac{42+20+13}{100} = \frac{75}{100} = $ **3/4** or **.75**.

Download additional solutions for free here:

www.thesatmathprep.com/28Les400.html

LESSON 13
HEART OF ALGEBRA

Reminder: Before beginning this lesson remember to redo the problems from Lessons 1, 5 and 9 that you have marked off. Do not "unmark" a question unless you get it correct.

Pick a Number

A problem may become much easier to understand and to solve by substituting a specific number in for a variable. Just make sure that you choose a number that satisfies the given conditions.

Here are some guidelines when picking numbers.

(1) Pick a number that is simple but not too simple. In general, you might want to avoid picking 0 or 1 (but 2 is usually a good choice).

(2) Try to avoid picking numbers that appear in the problem.

(3) When picking two or more numbers try to make them all different.

(4) Most of the time picking numbers only allows you to eliminate answer choices. So, do not just choose the first answer choice that comes out to the correct answer. If multiple answers come out correct you need to pick a new number and start again. But you only have to check the answer choices that have not yet been eliminated.

(5) If there are fractions in the question a good choice might be the least common denominator (lcd) or a multiple of the lcd.

(6) In percent problems choose the number 100.

(7) Do not pick a negative number as a possible answer to a grid-in question. This is a waste of time since you cannot grid a negative number.

(8) If your first attempt does not eliminate 3 of the 4 choices, try to choose a number that's of a different "type." Here are some examples of types:

    (a) A positive integer greater than 1.

    (b) A positive fraction (or decimal) between 0 and 1.

    (c) A negative integer less than -1.

    (d) A negative fraction (or decimal) between -1 and 0.

(9) If you are picking pairs of numbers, try different combinations from (8). For example, you can try two positive integers greater than 1, two negative integers less than -1, or one positive and one negative integer, etc.

Remember that these are just guidelines and there may be rare occasions where you might break these rules. For example, sometimes it is so quick and easy to plug in 0 and/or 1 that you might do this even though only some of the answer choices get eliminated.

Try to answer the following question using this strategy. **Do not** check the solution until you have attempted this question yourself.

LEVEL 1: HEART OF ALGEBRA

1.   A bank charges a fee of \$10 per month to have an account. In addition, there is a charge of \$0.05 per check written. Which of the following represents the total charge, in dollars, to have an account for one month in which n checks have been written?

    (A) $0.95n$
    (B) $1.05n$
    (C) $10.00 + 5n$
    (D) $10.00 + 0.05n$

Solution by picking a number: Let's choose a value for n, say $n = 4$. The total charge for the account including the checks written is then $\$10 + \$0.20 = \$10.20$. **Put a nice, big, dark circle around the number 10.20.** Now substitute 4 in for n in each answer choice and eliminate any answer that does not come out to 10.20.

    (A) 0.95(4) = 3.8
    (B) 1.05(4) = 4.2
    (C) 10.00 + 5(4) = 30
    (D) 10.00 + 0.05(4) = 10.20

Since choices (A), (B) and (C) came out incorrect, the answer is (D).

Before we go on, try to solve this problem algebraically.

* **Algebraic solution:** The total charge is \$10.00 for the account, plus \$0.05n for the checks. This is $10.00 + 0.05n$ dollars, choice (D).

Isolating a Variable in an Equation

On the SAT, you will sometimes be asked to solve for one variable in terms of others. Here is a simple example.

LEVEL 1: HEART OF ALGEBRA

$$C = \frac{5}{9}(F - 32)$$

2. The formula above shows how a temperature F, measured in degrees Fahrenheit, relates to a temperature C, measured in degrees Celsius. Which of the following gives F in terms of C ?

   (A) $F = \frac{5}{9}(C - 32)$

   (B) $F = \frac{9}{5}C + 32$

   (C) $F = \frac{9}{5}(C - 32)$

   (D) $F = \frac{9}{5}(C + 32)$

* **Algebraic solution:** To get F by itself we first multiply each side of the equation by $\frac{9}{5}$ to get $\frac{9}{5}C = F - 32$. We then add 32 to each side of the equation to get $\frac{9}{5}C + 32 = F$, or equivalently, $F = \frac{9}{5}C + 32$, choice (B).

You're doing great! Let's practice a bit more. Try to solve each of the following problems by picking a number. Then, if possible, solve each problem another way. The answers to these problems, followed by full solutions are at the end of this lesson. **Do not** look at the answers until you have attempted these problems yourself. Please remember to mark off any problems you get wrong.

LEVEL 1: HEART OF ALGEBRA

3. A caterer is hired to provide food for a private party consisting of 20 businessmen. She will be paid $80 per hour and an additional $40 tip if she serves all the food on time. If the caterer serves all the food on time, which of the following expressions can be used to determine how much the caterer earns, in dollars?

    (A) $40x + (80 + 20)$, where x is the number of businessmen
    (B) $(80 + 20)x + 40$, where x is the number of businessmen
    (C) $40x + 80$, where x is the number of hours
    (D) $80x + 40$, where x is the number of hours

4. Dawn is selling $5d$ CDs at a price of p dollars each. If x is the number of CDs she did <u>not</u> sell, which of the following represents the total dollar amount she received in sales from the CDs?

    (A) $px - 5d$
    (B) $5d - px$
    (C) $p(x - 5d)$
    (D) $p(5d - x)$

LEVEL 2: HEART OF ALGEBRA

5. David and John each ordered an entrée at a diner. The price of David's entrée was d dollars, and the price of John's entrée was $3 more than the price of David's entrée. If David and John split the cost of the entrees evenly and each paid an 18% tip, which of the following expressions represents the amount, in dollars, each of them paid? (Assume there is no sales tax.)

    (A) $2.36d + 3.54$
    (B) $1.18d + 1.77$
    (C) $1.50d + 0.18$
    (D) $.18d + 0.2$

LEVEL 3: HEART OF ALGEBRA

6. Which of the following is equal to $\frac{x+66}{22}$?

    (A) $\frac{x+33}{11}$

    (B) $x + 3$

    (C) $3x$

    (D) $\frac{x}{22} + 3$

Answers

1. D	4. D
2. B	5. B
3. D	6. D

Full Solutions

3.

Solution by picking a number: Let's choose a value for x, say $x = 2$. This means that the caterer worked for 2 hours. Since she makes $80 per hour, she made $80 \cdot 2 = 160$ dollars before receiving her tip. Since the caterer served all the food on time, she gets her tip of $40. So, the caterer earned a total of $160 + 40 = \mathbf{200}$ dollars.

Put a nice big dark circle around **200** so you can find it easier later. We now substitute $x = 2$ into each answer choice:

(A) $40 \cdot 2 + (80 + 20) = 80 + 100 = 180$
(B) $(80 + 20) \cdot 2 + 40 = 100 \cdot 2 + 40 = 200 + 40 = 240$
(C) $40 \cdot 2 + 80 = 80 + 80 = 160$
(D) $80 \cdot 2 + 40 = 160 + 40 = 200$

Since (A), (B), and (C) each came out incorrect, the answer is choice (D).

Important note: (D) is **not** the correct answer simply because it is equal to 200. It is correct because all three of the other choices are **not** 200. **You absolutely must check all four choices!**

Remark: All of the above computations can be done in a single step with your calculator (if a calculator is allowed for this problem).

* Algebraic solution: The caterer is being paid 80 dollars per hour, and she is working an unknown number of hours. So, we let x be the number of hours that the caterer is working. It follows that she makes $80x$ dollars, not including her tip. When we add in the 40 dollar tip, we see that the caterer will have earned a total of $80x + 40$ dollars, where x is the number of hours she worked, choice (D).

Notes: (1) Disregarding her tip, the caterer makes 80 dollars for 1 hour, $80 \cdot 2 = 160$ dollars for two hours, $80 \cdot 3 = 240$ dollars for 3 hours, and so on.

Following this pattern, we see that in general the caterer makes $80 \cdot x$ dollars, where x is the number of hours she worked.

(2) Don't forget to add in the tip of 40 dollars at the end to get a total of $80 \cdot x + 40$ dollars.

(3) The number of businessmen is not relevant in this problem. The caterer is being paid per hour, independent of the number of people at the party.

If instead she was being paid 80 dollars per businessman, then she would have been paid a fixed amount of $80 \cdot 20 = 1600$ dollars.

4.

Solution by picking numbers: Let's try $d = 4$, $p = 2$, $x = 5$. In this case Dawn is selling 20 CDs at a price of 2 dollars each. She did not sell 5 of them. Thus, she sold 15 of them and therefore she made $15 \cdot 2 = \mathbf{30}$ dollars. **Put a nice big, dark circle around this number so that you can find it easily later.** We now substitute the numbers that we chose into each answer choice.

(A) $2 * 5 - 5 * 4 = 10 - 20 = -10$
(B) $5 * 4 - 2 * 5 = 20 - 10 = 10$
(C) $2(5 - 5 * 4) = 2(5 - 20) = 2(-15) = -30$
(D) $2(5 * 4 - 5) = 2(20 - 5) = 2 * 15 = 30$

Since (A), (B) and (C) are incorrect we can eliminate them. Therefore, the answer is choice (D).

Important note: (D) is **not** the correct answer simply because it is equal to 30. It is correct because all 3 of the other choices are **not** 30.

Remark: It is not necessary to finish a computation if the answer is clearly incorrect. For example, in choice (C) we could stop at $2(5 - 20)$ since this is clearly a negative number, and we know that the answer is positive.

* Algebraic solution: Dawn sold $(5d - x)$ CDs ($5d$ is the total and x is the number she did not sell). Thus, the total dollar amount Dawn received in sales is $p(5d - x)$ (here p is the price per CD and $(5d - x)$ is the number of CDs that Dawn sold). Thus, the answer is choice (D).

5.
Solution by picking numbers: Let's try $d = 2$, so that the price of David's entrée was $2 and the price of John's entrée was $5. So, the total cost for the two entrées was $2 + 5 = 7, and the cost for each of them (before tip) was $3.50. We now add in the 18% tip. $.18(3.50) = .63$. So, each of them paid $3.50 + .63 = 4.13. **Put a nice big, dark circle around 4. 13 so that you can find it easily later.** We now substitute the numbers that we chose into each answer choice.

(A) $2.36 * 2 + 3.54 = 8.26$
(B) $1.18 * 2 + 1.77 = 4.13$
(C) $1.50 * 2 + 0.18 = 3.18$
(D) $.18 * 2 + 0.2 = 0.56$

Since (A), (C) and (D) are incorrect we can eliminate them. Therefore, the answer is choice (B).

Important note: (B) is **not** the correct answer simply because it is equal to 4.13. It is correct because all 3 of the other choices are **not** 4.13.

* Algebraic solution: John's entrée was $d + 3$ dollars, and so the total for the two entrees was $d + (d + 3) = 2d + 3$ dollars. When we add the 18% tip we get a total price of $1.18(2d + 3)$ dollars. Since they split the cost evenly, they each paid $.59(2d + 3) = 1.18d + 1.77$ dollars, choice (B).

6.
Solution by picking a number: Let's choose a value for x, say $x = 11$. We first substitute an 11 in for x into the given expression and use our calculator (if allowed). We type in the following: $(11 + 66)/22$ and we get $x = 3.5$. **Put a nice big, dark circle around this number so that you can find it easily later.** We now substitute 11 into each answer choice and use our calculator.

(A) $(11 + 33)/11 = 4$
(B) $11 + 3 = 14$
(C) $3*11 = 33$
(D) $11/22 + 3 = 3.5$

We now compare each of these numbers to the number that we put a nice big, dark circle around. Since (A), (B) and (C) are incorrect we can eliminate them. Therefore, the answer is choice (D).

Important note: (D) is **not** the correct answer simply because it is equal to 3.5. It is correct because all 3 of the other choices are **not** 3.5. **You absolutely must check all four choices!**

* **Algebraic solution:** Most students have no trouble at all adding two fractions with the same denominator. For example,

$$\frac{x}{22} + \frac{66}{22} = \frac{x + 66}{22}$$

But these same students have trouble reversing this process.

$$\frac{x + 66}{22} = \frac{x}{22} + \frac{66}{22}$$

Note that these two equations are **identical** except that the left and right hand sides have been switched. Note also that to break a fraction into two (or more) pieces, the original denominator is repeated for **each** piece.

An algebraic solution to the above problem consists of the following quick computation

$$\frac{x + 66}{22} = \frac{x}{22} + \frac{66}{22} = \frac{x}{22} + 3$$

This is choice (D).

LESSON 14
GEOMETRY

Reminder: Before beginning this lesson remember to redo the problems from Lessons 2, 6 and 10 that you have marked off. Do not "unmark" a question unless you get it correct.

Slope

The **slope** of a line is

$$\text{Slope} = m = \frac{rise}{run} = \frac{y_2 - y_1}{x_2 - x_1}$$

Lines with positive slope have graphs that go upwards from left to right. Lines with negative slope have graphs that go downwards from left to right. If the slope of a line is zero, it is horizontal. Vertical lines have **no** slope (also known as **infinite** slope or **undefined** slope).

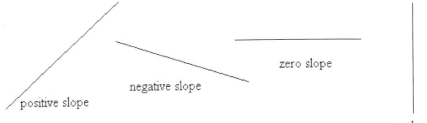

The **slope-intercept form of an equation of a line** is $y = mx + b$ where m is the slope of the line and b is the y-coordinate of the y-intercept, ie. the point $(0, b)$ is on the line. Note that this point lies on the y-axis.

Turn to page 94 and review **Pick a number**. Then try to answer the following question using this strategy. **Do not** check the solution until you have attempted this question yourself.

LEVEL 2: GEOMETRY

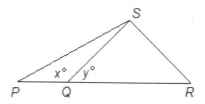

Note: Figure not drawn to scale.

1. In the figure above, point Q lies on side PR. If $49 < y < 51$, what is one possible value of x?

* Solution by picking a number: Let's choose a value for y, say $y = 50$. Then $x = 180 - 50 = \mathbf{130}$.

Remark: Angles PQS and SQR form a **linear pair**. This means that they are **supplementary**, i.e. their measures add up to 180 degrees. This is why $x = 180 - y$.

Complete geometric solution: $180 - 49 = 131$ and $180 - 51 = 129$. Therefore $129 < x < 131$. So, a possible answer is **130**.

Note: Although there are infinitely many solutions to this question, there is only one answer that will fit in the grid, namely 130.

Plug in the Given Point

If the graph of a function or other equation passes through certain points, plug those points into the equation to eliminate answer choices.

Try to answer the following question using this strategy. **Do not** check the solution until you have attempted this question yourself.

LEVEL 3: GEOMETRY

2. Which of the following is an equation of the line in the xy-plane that passes through the point $(0, -3)$ and is perpendicular to the line $y = \frac{1}{4}x + 7$?

    (A) $4x + y = -6$
    (B) $4x + y = -3$
    (C) $4x + y = 3$
    (D) $-x + 4y = 3$

* **Solution by plugging in the given point:** Since the point $(0, -3)$ lies on the line, if we substitute 0 in for x and -3 for y, we should get a true equation

    (A) $4 \cdot 0 - 3 = -6$ or $-3 = -6$ False
    (B) $4 \cdot 0 - 3 = -3$ or $-3 = -3$ True
    (C) $4 \cdot 0 - 3 = 3$ or $-3 = 3$ False
    (D) $-0 + 4(-3) = 3$ or $-12 = 3$ False

We can eliminate choices (A), (C) and (D) because they have become false. The answer is therefore choice (B).

Important note: (B) is **not** the correct answer simply because it came out true. It is correct because all 3 of the other choices were false.

Before we go on, try to solve this problem using geometry.

Geometric solution: Recall the slope-intercept form for the equation of a line: $y = mx + b$

$(0, -3)$ is the y-intercept of the line. Thus, $b = -3$. The slope of the given line is $\frac{1}{4}$. Since the new line is perpendicular to this line, its slope is -4, and the equation of the new line in slope-intercept form is $y = -4x - 3$.

We now add $4x$ to each side of this last equation to get $4x + y = -3$. This is choice (B).

Recall: Parallel lines have the same slope, and perpendicular lines have slopes that are negative reciprocals of each other.

You're doing great! Let's practice a bit more. Try to solve each of the following problems by picking numbers or plugging in points. Then, if possible, solve each problem another way. The answers to these problems, followed by full solutions are at the end of this lesson. **Do not** look at the answers until you have attempted these problems yourself. Please remember to mark off any problems you get wrong.

LEVEL 1: GEOMETRY

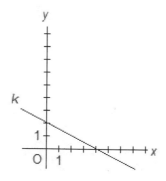

3.   What is the equation of line k in the figure above?

   (A) $y = -2x + 2$
   (B) $y = -2x + 4$
   (C) $y = -\dfrac{1}{2}x + 2$
   (D) $y = -\dfrac{1}{2}x + 4$

LEVEL 2: GEOMETRY

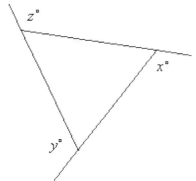

Note: Figure not drawn to scale.

4. In the figure above, what is the value of $x + y + z$?

LEVEL 3: GEOMETRY

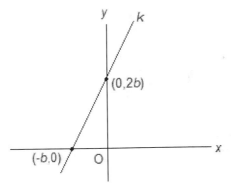

5. In the figure above, what is the slope of line k ?

106

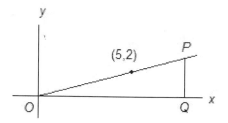

6. Line k (not shown) passes through O and intersects PQ between P and Q. What is one possible value of the slope of line k?

Answers

1. 130

2. B

3. C

4. 360

5. 2

6. $0 < m < .4$

Full Solutions

3.

Solution by plugging in the point: Since the point $(0, 2)$ lies on the line, if we substitute 0 in for x, we should get 2 for y. Let's substitute 0 in for x into each answer choice.

(A) 2
(B) 4
(C) 2
(D) 4

We can eliminate choices (B) and (D) because they did not come out to 2.

The point $(4, 0)$ also lies on the line. So, if we substitute 4 in for x, we should get 0 for y. Let's substitute 4 in for x in choices (A) and (C).

(A) $-2(4) + 2 = -8 + 2 = -6$
(C) $(-\frac{1}{2})(4) + 2 = -2 + 2 = 0$

We can eliminate choice (A) because it did not come out to 0. Therefore, the answer is choice (C).

* **Solution using the slope-intercept form of an equation of a line:** Recall that the slope-intercept form for the equation of a line is

$$y = mx + b.$$

$(0,2)$ is the y-intercept of the line. Thus, $b = 2$. The slope of the given line is $m = \dfrac{rise}{run} = -\dfrac{2}{4} = -\dfrac{1}{2}.$ Therefore, the equation of the line is $y = -\dfrac{1}{2}x + 2$, choice (C).

Note: To find the slope using the graph we simply note that to get from the y-intercept of the line to the x-intercept of the line we need to move down 2, then right 4

4.

Solution by picking numbers: Inside the triangle we can pick any 2 angles for free (just make sure that their sum is strictly less than 180). Here is an example:

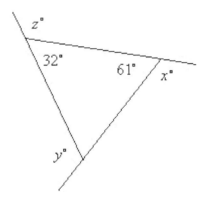

Since the angle measures of a triangle sum to 180, the other interior angle is

$$180 - 32 - 61 = 87 \text{ degrees.}$$

Furthermore, **the measure of an exterior angle to a triangle is the sum of the measures of the two opposite interior angles of the triangle.** So, we have

$$x = 87 + 32 = 119$$
$$y = 32 + 61 = \;\; 93$$
$$z = 87 + 61 = 148$$

So, $x + y + z = 119 + 93 + 148 = \mathbf{360}.$

Alternative: Each exterior angle of the triangle forms a **linear pair** with its adjacent interior angle, and therefore these two angles are **supplementary**. So $x + 61 = 180$, and therefore $x = 180 - 61 = 119$. Similarly, $y = 180 - 87 = 93$ and $z = 180 - 32 = 148$.

So, $x + y + z = 119 + 93 + 148 = \mathbf{360}$.

* Direct solution: A moment's thought will reveal that when we add x, y and z, we are adding each interior angle of the triangle twice (see bold text in the previous solution). Since there are 180 degrees in a triangle, the answer is $2 \cdot 180 = \mathbf{360}$.

Remark: We see from this solution that the answer to this problem is independent of what any of the interior angles are actually equal to.

5.

Solution by picking a number: Let's choose a value for b, say $b = 3$. Then the two points are $(-3, 0)$ and $(0, 6)$. The slope is $\frac{6-0}{0-(-3)} = \frac{6}{3} = \mathbf{2}$.

Remarks: (1) Here we have used the slope formula $m = \frac{y_2 - y_1}{x_2 - x_1}$.

(2) $0 - (-3) = 0 + 3 = 3$

(3) We could have also found the slope graphically by plotting the two points and observing that to get from $(-3, 0)$ to $(0, 6)$ we need to move up 6 and right 3. Thus, the slope is $m = \frac{rise}{run} = \frac{6}{3} = 2$.

* Solution using the slope formula: Let's use the formula for slope (as given in Remark (1) above). $\frac{2b-0}{0-(-b)} = \frac{2b}{b} = \mathbf{2}$.

6.

* Solution by picking a line: Let's choose a specific line k. The easiest choice is the line passing through $(0,0)$ and $(5,1)$. Now plug these two points into the slope formula to get $\frac{1-0}{5-0} = \mathbf{1/5}$.

Remarks: (1) Here we have used the slope formula $m = \frac{y_2 - y_1}{x_2 - x_1}$.

(2) If the line j passes through the origin (the point $(0,0)$) and the point (a, b) with $a \neq 0$, then the slope of line j is simply $\frac{b}{a}$.

Complete geometric solution: The slope of line OP is $\frac{2}{5} = .4$ (see Remark (2) above) and the slope of line OQ is 0. Therefore, we can choose any number strictly between 0 and .4 that fits in the answer grid.

LESSON 15
PASSPORT TO ADVANCED MATH

Reminder: Before beginning this lesson remember to redo the problems from Lessons 3, 7 and 11 that you have marked off. Do not "unmark" a question unless you get it correct.

The Distributive Property

The **distributive property** says that for all real numbers a, b, and c

$$a(b + c) = ab + ac$$

More specifically, this property says that the operation of multiplication distributes over addition. The distributive property is very important as it allows us to multiply and factor algebraic expressions.

Numeric example: Show that $2(3 + 4) = 2 \cdot 3 + 2 \cdot 4$

Solution: $2(3 + 4) = 2 \cdot 7 = 14$ and $2 \cdot 3 + 2 \cdot 4 = 6 + 8 = 14$.

Geometric Justification: The following picture gives a physical representation of the distributive property for this example.

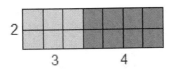

Note that the area of the light grey rectangle is $2 \cdot 3$, the area of the dark grey rectangle is $2 \cdot 4$, and the area of the whole rectangle is $2(3 + 4)$.

Algebraic examples: Use the distributive property to write each algebraic expression in an equivalent form.

(1) $2(x + 1)$ (2) $x(y - 3)$ (3) $-(x - y)$

Solutions: (1) $2(x + 1) = 2x + 2$

(2) $x(y - 3) = xy - 3x$

(3) $-(x - y) = -x + y$

Try this SAT math problem where the distributive property can be used.

LEVEL 1: ADVANCED MATH

$$5x(2y + z)$$

1. Which of the following is equivalent to the expression above?

    (A) $7xy + 5z$
    (B) $7xy + 5xz$
    (C) $10xy + xz$
    (D) $10xy + 5xz$

* Solution using the distributive property:

$$5x(2y + z) = 5x \cdot 2y + 5x \cdot z = 10xy + 5xz$$

So the answer is choice (D).

Note: (1) $5x \cdot 2y = 5 \cdot 2 \cdot x \cdot y = 10xy$. Similarly, $5x \cdot z = 5xz$.

Try to also solve this problem by picking numbers.

* Solution by picking numbers: Let's choose values for x, y, and z, say $x = 3$, $y = 4$, and $z = 6$. Then

$$5x(2y + z) = 5 \cdot 3(2 \cdot 4 + 6) = 15(8 + 6) = 15 \cdot 14 = \mathbf{210}.$$

Put a nice big, dark circle around this number so that you can find it easily later. We now substitute the numbers that we chose into each answer choice.

    (A) $7 * 3 * 4 + 5 * 6 = 114$
    (B) $7 * 3 * 4 + 5 * 3 * 6 = 174$
    (C) $10 * 3 * 4 + 3 * 6 = 138$
    (D) $10 * 3 * 4 + 5 * 3 * 6 = 210$

Since (A), (B) and (C) are incorrect we can eliminate them. Therefore, the answer is choice (D).

Important note: (D) is **not** the correct answer simply because it is equal to 210. It is correct because all 3 of the other choices are **not** 210.

Factoring

When we use the distributive property in the opposite direction, we usually call it **factoring**.

Examples: (1) $2x + 4y = 2(x + 2y)$

(2) $3x + 5xy = x(3 + 5y)$

(3) $6xy + 9yz = 3y(2x + 3z)$

Try this SAT math problem that can be solved by factoring.

LEVEL 1: ADVANCED MATH

2.   If $10xz - 15yz = az(2x - by)$ where a and b are positive real numbers, what is the value of $a + b$?

* Solution by factoring:

$$10xz - 15yz = 5z(2x - 3y)$$

So $a = 5, b = 3$, and therefore $a + b = 5 + 3 = $ **8**.

Advanced Factoring

The Difference of Two Squares: $a^2 - b^2 = (a - b)(a + b)$

Examples: (1) $x^2 - 9 = (x - 3)(x + 3)$
(2) $4x^2 - 25y^2 = (2x - 5y)(2x + 5y)$
(3) $36 - 49x^2y^2 = (6 - 7xy)(6 + 7xy)$

Trinomial Factoring: $x^2 - (a + b)x + ab = (x - a)(x - b)$

Examples: (1) $x^2 - 5x + 6 = (x - 2)(x - 3)$

(2) $x^2 - 2x - 35 = (x - 7)(x + 5)$

(3) $x^2 + 14x + 33 = (x + 3)(x + 11)$

LEVEL 3: ADVANCED MATH

$$16b^2 - 4a^2$$

3.   Which of the following is equivalent to the expression above?

(A) $(4b - 2a)^2$
(B) $(4b + 2a)^2$
(C) $(b - a)(16b + 4a)$
(D) $(4b - 2a)(4b + 2a)$

* Solution using the difference of two squares:

$$16b^2 - 4a^2 = (4b - 2a)(4b + 2a), \text{ choice (D)}.$$

Notes: (1) The positive square root of $16b^2$ is $4b$, and the positive square root of $4a^2$ is $2a$.

(2) This problem can also be solved by picking numbers. I leave this solution to the reader.

You're doing great! Let's just practice a bit more. Try to solve each of the following problems by using one of the techniques you just learned. The answers to these problems, followed by full solutions are at the end of this lesson. **Do not** look at the answers until you have attempted these problems yourself. Please remember to mark off any problems you get wrong.

LEVEL 2: ADVANCED MATH

4. What is the value of $d - 2$ if $(6d - 3) - (2 - d) = 9$?

5. The expression $x^2 + 2x - 35$ can be written as the product of two binomial factors with integer coefficients. One of the binomials is $(x + 7)$. If the other binomial is $(x - b)$, what is the value of b ?

LEVEL 3: ADVANCED MATH

$$16x^6 + 40x^3y^2 + 25y^4$$

6. Which of the following is equivalent to the expression above?

(A) $(4x^3 + 5y^2)^2$
(B) $(4x^2 + 5y)^4$
(C) $(16x^3 + 25y^2)^2$
(D) $(16x^2 + 25y)^4$

Answers

1. D	4. 0
2. 8	5. 5
3. D	6. A

Full Solutions

4.

* Solution using the distributive property:

$$(6d - 3) - (2 - d) = 6d - 3 - 2 + d = 7d - 5$$

So, the given equation is equivalent to $7d - 5 = 9$. We add 5 to each side of this last equation to get $7d = 9 + 5 = 14$. We then divide by 7 to get $d = \frac{14}{7} = 2$. So $d - 2 = 2 - 2 = \mathbf{0}$.

5.

* Algebraic solution: We are being asked to factor $x^2 + 2x - 35$. But we are also given that one of the factors is $(x + 7)$. Since $-\frac{35}{7} = -5$, the other factor must be $(x - 5)$, and so $b = \mathbf{5}$.

Notes: (1) On the SAT, an expression of the form $x^2 + bx + c$ will usually factor as $(x + m)(x + n)$ where m and n are integers and $m \cdot n = c$.

In this problem, $c = -35$ and $m = 7$. So $n = -\frac{35}{7} = -5$.

(2) A **binomial** has two terms. For example, the two terms of $(x + 7)$ are x and 7. The two terms of $(x - 5)$ are x and -5.

Solution by picking a number: Let's choose a value for x, say $x = 0$. Then $x^2 + 2x - 35 = -35$, $(x + 7) = 7$, and $(x - b) = -b$. So, we have $-35 = 7(-b) = -7b$, and so $b = \frac{-35}{-7} = \mathbf{5}$.

Note: By picking the number $x = 0$, we have changed the problem to "the number -35 can be written as a product of 7 and what other number?" The other number is $-b = -5$, and so $b = 5$.

6.

* Solution using trinomial factoring:

$$16x^6 + 40x^3y^2 + 25y^4 = (4x^3 + 5y^2)(4x^3 + 5y^2) = (4x^3 + 5y^2)^2$$

This is choice (A).

Note: This problem can also be solved by picking numbers (try $x = y = 1$). I leave this solution to the reader.

LESSON 16
PROBLEM SOLVING

Reminder: Before beginning this lesson remember to redo the problems from Lessons 4, 8 and 12 that you have marked off. Do not "unmark" a question unless you get it correct.

Percent Change

Memorize the following simple formula for percent change problems.

$$Percent\ Change = \frac{Change}{Original} \times 100$$

Note that this is the same formula for both a percent increase and a percent decrease problem.

Try to answer the following question using this strategy. **Do not** check the solution until you have attempted this question yourself.

LEVEL 2: PROBLEM SOLVING

1. In September, Daniela was able to type 30 words per minute. In October, she was able to type 42 words per minute. By what percent did Daniela's speed increase from September to October?

   (A) 12%
   (B) 18%
   (C) 30%
   (D) 40%

* This is a percent increase problem. So, we will use the formula for percent change.

The **original** value is 30. The new value is 42, so that the **change** is 12. Using the percent change formula, we get that the percent increase is $\frac{12}{30} \cdot 100 = 40\%$, choice (D).

Warning: Do not accidently use the new value for "change" in the formula. The **change** is the positive difference between the original and new values.

Setting Up a Ratio

Step 1: Identify two key words and write them down one over the other.

Step 2: Next to each of these key words write down the numbers, variables or expressions that correspond to each key word in two columns.

Step 3: Draw in 2 division symbols and an equal sign.

Step 4: Cross multiply and divide.

Try to answer the following question using this strategy. **Do not** check the solution until you have attempted this question yourself.

LEVEL 1: PROBLEM SOLVING

2. The sales tax on a $5.00 hat is $0.40. At this rate, what would be the sales tax on a $9.00 hat? (Disregard the percent symbol when gridding in your answer.)

* This is a simple ratio. We begin by identifying 2 key words that tell us what 2 things are being compared. In this case, such a pair of key words is "hat" and "tax."

$$
\begin{array}{ccc}
\text{hat} & 5 & 9 \\
\text{tax} & 0.40 & x
\end{array}
$$

Choose the words that are most helpful to you. Notice that we wrote in the hat prices next to the word hat, and the tax prices next to the word tax. Also, notice that the tax for a $5 hat is written under the number 5, and the (unknown) tax for a $9 hat is written under the 9. Now draw in the division symbols and equal sign, cross multiply and divide the corresponding ratio to find the unknown quantity x.

$$\frac{5}{0.40} = \frac{9}{x}$$
$$5x = (9)(0.40)$$
$$5x = 3.6$$
$$x = \frac{3.6}{5} = 0.72$$

So, the tax on a $9 hat is $0.72. So, we grid in . **72**.

Change Fractions to Decimals

Decimals are often easier to work with than fractions when a calculator is allowed. To change a fraction to a decimal you simply perform the division in your calculator.

Try to answer the following question using this strategy. **Do not** check the solution until you have attempted this question yourself.

LEVEL 1: PROBLEM SOLVING

3.   * Which of the following numbers is between $\frac{1}{9}$ and $\frac{1}{8}$?

     (A) 0.10
     (B) 0.12
     (C) 0.14
     (D) 0.16

* Change the two fractions to decimals by dividing in your calculator. Dividing 1 by 9 gives about 0.1111. Dividing 1 by 8 gives .125. Since 0.12 is between these two the answer is choice (B).

Now try to solve each of the following problems involving percents and ratios. The answers to these problems, followed by full solutions are at the end of this lesson. **Do not** look at the answers until you have attempted these problems yourself. Please remember to mark off any problems you get wrong.

LEVEL 1: PROBLEM SOLVING

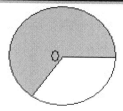

4. O is the center of the circle above. Approximately what percent of the circle is shaded?

     (A) 37%
     (B) 50%
     (C) 67%
     (D) 75%

LEVEL 2: PROBLEM SOLVING

5.   * What percent of 75 is 32? (Disregard the percent symbol when gridding in your answer.

6.   The ratio of 17 to 3 is equal to the ratio of 102 to what number?

LEVEL 3: PROBLEM SOLVING

7.   Marco is drawing a time line to represent a 500-year period of time. If he makes the time line 80 inches long and draws it to scale, how many inches will represent each year?

8.   During a sale at a retail store, if a customer buys one t-shirt at full price, the customer is given a 40 percent discount on a second t-shirt of equal or lesser value. If John buys two t-shirts that have full prices of $70 and $90, by what percent is the total cost of the two t-shirts reduced during the sale? (Disregard the percent symbol when you grid your answer.)

Answers

1. D	5. 42.6 or 42.7
2. .72	6. 18
3. B	7. 4/25 or .16
4. C	8. 17.5

Full Solutions

4.

* More than half (50%) of the circle is shaded, and less than $\frac{3}{4}$ (75%) is shaded. So, the answer must be 67%, choice (C).

5.

* The word "what" indicates an unknown, let's call it x. The word percent means "out of 100" or "divided by 100." The word "of" indicates multiplication, and the word "is" indicates an equal sign. So, we translate the given sentence into an algebraic equation as follows.

$$\frac{x}{100} \cdot 75 = 32$$

So, $x = 32 \left(\frac{100}{75}\right) \approx 42.6667$. So, we grid in **42.6** or **42.7**.

6.

*

$$\frac{17}{3} = \frac{102}{x}$$
$$17x = 306$$
$$x = \textbf{18}$$

7.

* This is a simple ratio. We begin by identifying 2 key words that tell us what 2 things are being compared. In this case, such a pair of key words is "years" and "inches."

years	500	1
inches	80	x

Now draw in the division symbols and equal sign, cross multiply and divide the corresponding ratio to find the unknown quantity x.

$$\frac{500}{80} = \frac{1}{x}$$
$$500x = (1)(80)$$
$$x = \frac{80}{500} = .16$$

So we can grid in **.16** or the fraction **4/25**.

8.

* This is a percent decrease problem. So, we will use the formula for percent change. The **original** cost of the two t-shirts is $70 + 90 = 160$. The new cost is $42 + 90 = 132$. Thus, the **change** is $160 - 132 = 28$. So, the percent change is $\left(\frac{28}{160}\right) \cdot 100 = 17.5\%$. So, we grid in the answer **17.5**.

Note: To get the 42 in the second computation we need to discount 70 by 40 percent. Here are two ways to do that.

(1) Compute 40% of 70:. $4 \cdot 70 = 28$. Then subtract $70 - 28 = 42$.
(2) Compute 60% of 70:. $6 \cdot 70 = 42$ (taking a 40% discount of something is the same as taking 60% of that thing).

Warning: Do not accidently use the new value for "change" in the formula. The **change** is the positive difference between the original and new values.

OPTIONAL MATERIAL

The following questions will test your understanding of definitions used in this lesson. These are **not** SAT questions.

1. Convert each fraction to a decimal and a percent (round each result to two decimal places).

$$\frac{1}{2} \qquad \frac{1}{5} \qquad \frac{1}{3} \qquad 1 \qquad \frac{5}{3}$$

2. Convert each decimal to a percent and a reduced fraction.

$$.5 \qquad .24 \qquad 1 \qquad 1.5 \qquad 12$$

3. Convert each percent to a decimal and a reduced fraction.

$$5\% \qquad .3\% \qquad .07\% \qquad 15\% \qquad 100\%$$

Answers

1. $\frac{1}{2} = .5 = 50\%, \frac{1}{5} = .2 = 20\%, \frac{1}{3} = .33 = 33.33\%,$
   $1 = 1 = 100\%, \frac{5}{3} = 1.67 = 166.67\%$

2. $.5 = 50\% = \frac{1}{2}, .24 = 24\% = \frac{6}{25}, 1 = 100\% = 1,$
   $1.5 = 150\% = \frac{3}{2}, 12 = 1200\% = 12$

3. $5\% = .05 = \frac{1}{20}, .3\% = .003 = \frac{3}{1000}, .07\% = .0007 = \frac{7}{10,000},$
   $15\% = .15 = \frac{3}{20}, 100\% = 1 = 1$

LESSON 17
HEART OF ALGEBRA

Reminder: Before beginning this lesson remember to redo the problems from Lessons 1, 5, 9 and 13 that you have marked off. Do not "unmark" a question unless you get it correct.

Try a Simple Operation

Problems that ask for an expression involving more than one variable often look much harder than they are. By performing a single operation, the problem is usually reduced to one that is very easy to solve. The most common operations to try are addition, subtraction, multiplication and division.

Try to answer the following question using this strategy. **Do not** check the solution until you have attempted this question yourself.

LEVEL 2: ALGEBRA

1. If $7x + y = 6$ and $5x + y = 2$, what is the value of $6x + y$?

    (A) -8
    (B)   4
    (C)   6
    (D) 12

* Solution by trying a simple operation: We add the two equations:

$$7x + y = 6$$
$$\underline{5x + y = 2}$$
$$12x + 2y = 8$$

Now observe that $12x + 2y = 2(6x + y)$. So $6x + y = \frac{8}{2} = 4$, choice (B).

Before we go on, try to solve this problem the way you would do it in school.

Solution using the elimination method: We subtract the two equations to isolate x

121

$$7x + y = 6$$
$$\underline{5x + y = 2}$$
$$2x \quad\;\;= 4$$

So $x = 2$. Substituting $x = 2$ back into the first equation we get

$$7(2) + y = 6$$
$$14 + y = 6$$
$$y = -8$$

So, $6x + y = 6(2) - 8 = 12 - 8 = 4$, choice (B).

Recognize Blocks

We define a **block** to be an algebraic expression that appears more than once in a given problem. Very often in SAT problems a block can be treated just like a variable. In particular, blocks should usually not be manipulated—treat them as a single unit.

Try to answer the following question using this strategy. **Do not** check the solution until you have attempted this question yourself.

LEVEL 1: ALGEBRA

2.   If $3(a + b) - 4 = 41$, then $a + b =$

* Solution by recognizing a block: There is a block of $a + b$. Let's look at a seemingly easier problem:

If $3x - 4 = 41$, then $x =$

We can guess values for x until we get the right answer.

x	$3x - 4$	
20	$3*20 - 4 = 60 - 4 = 56$	too big
12	$3*12 - 4 = 36 - 4 = 32$	too small
15	$3*15 - 4 = 45 - 4 = 41$	correct

Thus, the answer is **15**.

But this is essentially the same problem as the one we were given. We just replaced the block by the variable x. So, the answer to the original question is also **15**.

Alternative: Instead of guessing values for x, we can simply perform the algebra.

$$3x - 4 = 41$$
$$3x = 45$$
$$x = \mathbf{15}.$$

Before we go on, try to solve this problem quickly by doing informal algebra in your head.

* Mental math: Simply add 4 to 41, and then divide by 3 to get the answer.

$$a + b = \frac{41 + 4}{3} = \frac{45}{3} = \mathbf{15}.$$

You're doing great! Let's just practice a bit more. Try to solve each of the following problems by using one of the strategies you just learned. Then, if possible, solve each problem another way. The answers to these problems, followed by full solutions are at the end of this lesson. **Do not** look at the answers until you have attempted these problems yourself. Please remember to mark off any problems you get wrong.

LEVEL 2: ALGEBRA

3. If $x + 7y = 15$ and $x + 3y = 7$, what is the value of $x + 5y$?

4. If $\frac{a+3}{5} = 20$ and $\frac{a+b}{12} = 10$, what is the value of b?

5. If $3x - 5y = 7$, what is the value of $6(3x - 5y)$?

   (A) 50
   (B) 42
   (C) 36
   (D) 30

LEVEL 3: ALGEBRA

6. If $21x + 49y = 28$, what is the value of $3x + 7y$?

123

Answers

1. B   4. 23
2. 15   5. B
3. 11   6. 4

Full Solutions

3.

* Solution by trying a simple operation: We add the two equations

$$x + 7y = 15$$
$$\underline{x + 3y = 7}$$
$$2x + 10y = 22$$

Now observe that $2x + 10y = 2(x + 5y)$. So $x + 5y = \frac{22}{2} = \mathbf{11}$.

4.

* Solution by trying a simple operation: We begin by multiplying each side of the first equation by 5, and each side of the second equation by 12 to eliminate the denominators.

$$a + 3 = 100$$
$$a + b = 120$$

Now subtract the first equation from the second equation.

$$a + b = 120$$
$$\underline{a + 3 = 100}$$
$$b - 3 = 20$$

Finally, add 3 to each side of the resulting equation to get $b = \mathbf{23}$.

5.

* Solution by recognizing a block: In this example, there is a block of $\mathbf{3x - 5y}$. Let's look at the following seemingly easier problem:

If $a = 7$, what is the value of $6a$?

The answer to this problem is $(6)(7) = 42$.

But this is essentially the same problem as the one we were given. We just replaced the block by the variable a. So, the answer to the original question is also 42, choice (B).

* **Mental math:** This problem can be done in just a few seconds.

$$(6)(7) = 42, \text{ choice (B)}.$$

6.

* **Solution by trying a simple operation:** We divide each side of the equation by 7 to get $3x + 7y = 4$.

Note: When we divide the left-hand side by 7, we have to divide **each** term by 7.

$$\frac{21x}{7} = 3x \qquad\qquad \frac{49y}{7} = 7y$$

Alternative: We can factor out 7 on the left-hand side

$$21x + 49y = 7(3x + 7y).$$

So we have

$$21x + 49y = 28$$
$$7(3x + 7y) = 28$$
$$3x + 7y = \frac{28}{7} = 4.$$

Download additional solutions for free here:

www.thesatmathprep.com/28Les400.html

LESSON 18
GEOMETRY AND TRIGONOMETRY

Reminder: Before beginning this lesson remember to redo the problems from Lessons 2, 6, 10 and 14 that you have marked off. Do not "unmark" a question unless you get it correct.

The Pythagorean Theorem

The Pythagorean Theorem says that if a right triangle has legs of length a and b, and a hypotenuse of length c, then $c^2 = a^2 + b^2$. Note that the Pythagorean Theorem is one of the formulas given to you in the beginning of each math section.

Try to answer the following question using the Pythagorean Theorem. **Do not** check the solution until you have attempted this question yourself.

LEVEL 1: GEOMETRY

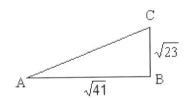

Note: Figure not drawn to scale.

1.   In right triangle ABC above, what is the length of side AC ?

* **Solution using the Pythagorean Theorem:** We use the Pythagorean Theorem: $c^2 = a^2 + b^2 = 23 + 41 = 64$. Therefore $AC = c = \mathbf{8}$.

Right Triangle Trigonometry

Let's consider the following right triangle, and let's focus our attention on angle A.

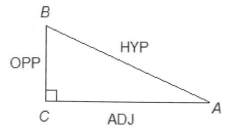

Note that the **hypotenuse** is ALWAYS the side opposite the right angle.

The other two sides of the right triangle, called the **legs**, depend on which angle is chosen. In this picture, we chose to focus on angle A. Therefore, the opposite side is BC, and the adjacent side is AC.

It's worth memorizing how to compute the three basic trig functions:

$$\sin A = \frac{\text{OPP}}{\text{HYP}} \qquad \cos A = \frac{\text{ADJ}}{\text{HYP}} \qquad \tan A = \frac{\text{OPP}}{\text{ADJ}}$$

Here is a tip to help you remember these:

Many students find it helpful to use the word SOHCAHTOA. You can think of the letters here as representing sin, opp, hyp, cos, adj, hyp, tan, opp, adj.

Example: Compute the three basic trig functions for each of the angles (except the right angle) in the triangle below.

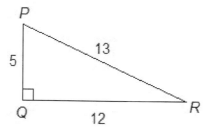

Solution:

$$\sin P = \frac{12}{13} \qquad \cos P = \frac{5}{13} \qquad \tan P = \frac{12}{5}$$

$$\sin R = \frac{5}{13} \qquad \cos R = \frac{12}{13} \qquad \tan R = \frac{5}{12}$$

LEVEL 2: TRIGONOMETRY

2. If $0 \leq x \leq 90°$ and $\cos x = \frac{5}{13}$, then $\tan x =$

* Trigonometric solution: Let's draw a picture. We begin with a right triangle and label one of the angles x.

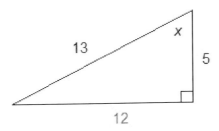

Since $\cos x = \frac{\text{ADJ}}{\text{HYP}}$, we label the leg adjacent to x with a 5 and the hypotenuse with 13. We can use the Pythagorean triple 5, 12, 13 to see that the other side is 12.

Finally, $\tan x = \frac{\text{OPP}}{\text{ADJ}} = \mathbf{12/5}$ or $\mathbf{2.4}$.

Notes: (1) The most common Pythagorean triples are 3, 4, 5 and 5, 12, 13. Two others that may come up are 8, 15, 17 and 7, 24, 25.

(2) If you don't remember the Pythagorean triple 5, 12, 13, you can use the Pythagorean Theorem:

Here we have $5^2 + b^2 = 13^2$. Therefore $25 + b^2 = 169$. Subtracting 25 from each side of this equation gives $b^2 = 169 - 25 = 144$. So $b = 12$.

(3) The equation $b^2 = 144$ would normally have two solutions: $b = 12$ and $b = -12$. But the length of a side of a triangle cannot be negative, so we reject -12.

Cofunction Identities

$$\sin(90° - x) = \cos x \qquad \cos(90° - x) = \sin x$$

LEVEL 3: TRIGONOMETRY

3.   In a right triangle, one angle measures $x°$, where $\cos x° = \frac{2}{3}$. What is $\sin((90-x)°)$?

* Solution using a cofunction identity: $\sin((90-x)°) = \cos x° = \mathbf{2/3}$.

If we were to encounter this problem, and we do not remember the cofunction identity, we can also solve this problem with a picture and some basic trigonometry.

Basic trig solution: Let's draw a picture:

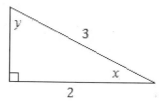

Notice that I labeled one of the angles with x, and used the fact that $\cos x = \frac{\text{ADJ}}{\text{HYP}}$ to label 2 sides of the triangle.

Now observe that $y° = (90-x)°$, so that

$$\sin((90-x)°) = \sin y° = \frac{\text{OPP}}{\text{HYP}} = \mathbf{2/3}.$$

You're doing great! Let's just practice a bit more. Try to solve each of the following problems. The answers to these problems, followed by full solutions are at the end of this lesson. **Do not** look at the answers until you have attempted these problems yourself. Please remember to mark off any problems you get wrong.

LEVEL 1: GEOMETRY AND TRIG

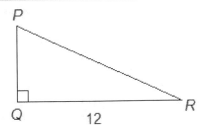

4.   In $\triangle PQR$ above, $\tan R = \frac{5}{12}$. What is the length of side PR?

LEVEL 3: GEOMETRY AND TRIG

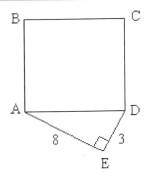

5.   In the figure above, what is the area of square $ABCD$?

6.   In a right triangle, one angle measures $x°$, where $\sin x° = \frac{3}{5}$. What is $\cos((90-x)°)$?

Answers

1. 8
2. 12/5 or 2.4
3. 2/3, .666, or .667

4. 13
5. 73
6. 3/5 or .6

Full Solutions

4.

* Since $\tan R = \frac{\text{OPP}}{\text{ADJ}}$, we have $\frac{5}{12} = \frac{\text{OPP}}{\text{ADJ}}$. Since the adjacent side is 12, the opposite side must be 5. So we have the following picture.

130

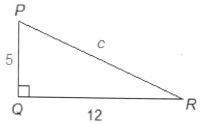

We now find PR by using the Pythagorean Theorem, or better yet, recognizing the Pythagorean triple 5, 12, 13. So PR = **13**.

Remarks: (1) If you don't remember the Pythagorean triple 5, 12, 13, you can use the Pythagorean Theorem. In this problem, we have $c^2 = 5^2 + 12^2 = 169$. So $c = 13$.

(2) The equation $c^2 = 169$ would normally have two solutions: $c = 13$ and $c = -13$. But the length of a side of a triangle cannot be negative, so we reject -13.

5.
* Let x be the length of a side of the square. So $AD = x$. We now use the Pythagorean Theorem.

$$x^2 = 8^2 + 3^2 = 64 + 9 = 73.$$

But x^2 is precisely the area of the square. Therefore, the answer is **73**.

6.
Basic trig solution: Let's draw a picture:

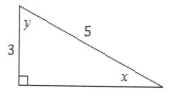

Notice that I labeled one of the angles with x, and used the fact that $\sin x = \frac{\text{OPP}}{\text{HYP}}$ to label 2 sides of the triangle.

Now observe that $y° = (90 - x)°$, so that

$$\cos((90 - x)°) = \cos y° = \frac{\text{ADJ}}{\text{HYP}} = \mathbf{3/5} \text{ or } \mathbf{.6}.$$

* **Solution using a cofunction identity:** $\cos((90 - x)°) = \sin x° = \mathbf{3/5}$.

131

LESSON 19
PASSPORT TO ADVANCED MATH

Reminder: Before beginning this lesson remember to redo the problems from Lessons 3, 7, 11 and 15 that you have marked off. Do not "unmark" a question unless you get it correct.

Addition and Subtraction of Polynomials

We add polynomials by simply combining like terms. We can change any subtraction problem to an addition problem by first distributing the minus sign. Let's look at an example.

LEVEL 2: ADVANCED MATH

$$(-3x^2 + 2x) - (-3x^2 - 2x)$$

1. Which of the following is equivalent to the expression above?

> (A) 0
> (B) $-6x^2$
> (C) $4x$
> (D) $-6x^2 + 4x$

* Algebraic solution:

$$(-3x^2 + 2x) - (-3x^2 - 2x)$$
$$= -3x^2 + 2x + 3x^2 + 2x$$
$$= (-3x^2 + 3x^2) + (2x + 2x) = 0 + 4x = 4x$$

This is choice (C).

Multiplication of Polynomials

Most students are familiar with the mnemonic FOIL to help them multiply two binomials (polynomials with 2 terms) together. As a simple example, we have

$$(x + 1)(x - 2) = x^2 - 2x + x - 2 = x^2 - x - 2$$

Unfortunately, this method works ONLY for binomials. It does not extend to polynomials with more than 2 terms. Let's demonstrate another way to multiply polynomials with the same example.

We begin by lining up the polynomials vertically:

$$x + 1$$
$$\underline{x - 2}$$

We multiply the -2 on the bottom by each term on top, moving from right to left. First note that -2 times 1 is -2:

$$x + 1$$
$$\underline{x - 2}$$
$$-2$$

Next note that -2 times x is $-2x$:

$$x + 1$$
$$\underline{x - 2}$$
$$-2x - 2$$

Now we multiply the x on the bottom by each term on top, moving from right to left. This time as we write the answers we leave one blank space on the right:

$$x + 1$$
$$\underline{x - 2}$$
$$-2x - 2$$
$$\underline{x^2 + x}$$

Finally, we add:

$$x + 1$$
$$\underline{x - 2}$$
$$-2x - 2$$
$$\underline{x^2 + x}$$
$$x^2 - x - 2$$

Try to use this algorithm to solve the following problem.

LEVEL 2: ADVANCED MATH

2. The expression $(3b - 2)(b + 5)$ is equivalent to:

(A) $3b^2 - 7$
(B) $3b^2 - 10$
(C) $3b^2 - 2b - 7$
(D) $3b^2 + 13b - 10$

* Algebraic solution:

$$
\begin{array}{r}
3b - 2 \\
\underline{b + 5} \\
15b - 10 \\
\underline{3b^2 - 2b} \\
3b^2 + 13b - 10
\end{array}
$$

This is choice (D).

You're doing great! Let's just practice a bit more. Try to solve each of the following problems by using one of the techniques you just learned. The answers to these problems, followed by full solutions are at the end of this lesson. **Do not** look at the answers until you have attempted these problems yourself. Please remember to mark off any problems you get wrong.

LEVEL 2: ADVANCED MATH

$$5(3x - 2)(2x + 1)$$

3. Which of the following is equivalent to the expression above?

     (A) $30x^2 - 10$
     (B) $30x^2 - 5x - 10$
     (C) $25x^2 - 20$
     (D) $15x$

$$3(-2x^3 + 5x^2 - x + 1) - 3(x^3 - 2x^2 - 5x - 2)$$

4. If we write the above expression in the form $ax^3 + bx^2 + cx + d$, where a, b, c, and d are constants, what is the value of c ?

LEVEL 3: ADVANCED MATH

5. What polynomial must be added to $x^2 + 3x - 5$ so that the sum is $5x^2 - 8$?

     (A) $4x^2 - 5x + 6$
     (B) $4x^2 - 3x - 3$
     (C) $5x^2 - 3x - 3$
     (D) $5x^2 + 3x + 6$

6. For all x, $(x^2 - 3x + 1)(x + 2) = ?$

    (A) $x^3 - x^2 - 5x + 2$
    (B) $x^3 - x^2 - 5x - 2$
    (C) $x^3 - x^2 + 5x + 2$
    (D) $x^3 + x^2 - 5x + 2$

Answers

    1. C   4. 12
    2. D   5. B
    3. B   6. A

Full Solutions

3.
* $5(3x - 2)(2x + 1) = 5(6x^2 + 3x - 4x - 2) = 5(6x^2 - x - 2)$
$$= 30x^2 - 5x - 10$$

This is choice (B).

Note: We can multiply $(3x - 2)$ and $(2x + 1)$ either by using FOIL or by using the algorithm given in this lesson.

4.
* Since c is the coefficient of x, we simply compute

$$3(-x) - 3(-5x) = -3x + 15x = 12x.$$

It follows that $c = $ **12**.

Complete algebraic solution:

$$3(-2x^3 + 5x^2 - x + 1) - 3(x^3 - 2x^2 - 5x - 2)$$
$$= -6x^3 + 15x^2 - 3x + 3 - 3x^3 + 6x^2 + 15x + 6$$
$$= (-6x^3 - 3x^3) + (15x^2 + 6x^2) + (-3x + 15x) + (3 + 6)$$
$$= -9x^3 + 21x^2 + 12x + 9$$

So $a = -9$, $b = 21$, $c = 12$, and $d = 9$.

In particular, $c = $ **12**.

5.
* **Algebraic solution:** We need to subtract $(5x^2 - 8) - (x^2 + 3x - 5)$.
We first eliminate the parentheses by distributing the minus sign:

135

$$5x^2 - 8 - x^2 - 3x + 5$$

Finally, we combine like terms to get $4x^2 - 3x - 3$, choice (B).

Remark: Pay careful attention to the minus and plus signs in the solution above. In particular, make sure you are distributing correctly.

6.

* Algebraic solution: We multiply the two polynomials.

$$
\begin{array}{r}
x^2 - 3x + 1 \\
x + 2 \\
\hline
2x^2 - 6x + 2 \\
x^3 - 3x^2 + x + 0 \\
\hline
x^3 - x^2 - 5x + 2
\end{array}
$$

This is choice (A).

Download additional solutions for free here:

www.thesatmathprep.com/28Les400.html

LESSON 20
STATISTICS

Reminder: Before beginning this lesson remember to redo the problems from Lessons 4, 8, 12 and 16 that you have marked off. Do not "unmark" a question unless you get it correct.

Basic Statistics

The **average (arithmetic mean)** of a list of numbers is the sum of the numbers in the list divided by the quantity of the numbers in the list.

$$\textbf{Average} = \frac{\textbf{Sum}}{\textbf{Number}}$$

The **median** of a list of numbers is the middle number when the numbers are arranged in increasing order. If the total number of values in the list is even, then the median is the average of the two middle values.

The **mode** of a list of numbers is the number that occurs most frequently. There can be more than one mode if more than one number occurs with the greatest frequency.

The **standard deviation** of a set of numbers measures how far the numbers are from the arithmetic mean.

Example 1: Let's compute the average (arithmetic mean), median, and mode of 2, 3, 7, 5, 1, 7, 3.

$$\text{Average} = \frac{2+3+7+5+1+7+3}{7} = \frac{28}{7} = 4$$

To find the median it is helpful to rewrite the numbers in increasing order: 1, 2, 3, 3, 5, 7, 7. Then the median is 3.

There are 2 modes: 3 and 7.

Turn to page 36 and review **Change averages to sums.** Then try to solve each of the following problems using this strategy whenever possible. The answers to these problems are at the end of this lesson. **Do not** look at the answers until you have attempted these problems yourself. If you are getting any of these questions wrong, go back and redo Lesson 4.

LEVEL 1: STATISTICS

1. The average (arithmetic mean) of four numbers is 80. If three of the numbers are 32, 62 and 82, what is the fourth number?

2. For which of the following lists of 5 numbers is the average (arithmetic mean) less than the median?

   (A) 2, 2, 4, 5, 5
   (B) 2, 3, 4, 6, 7
   (C) 2, 2, 4, 6, 6
   (D) 2, 3, 4, 5, 6

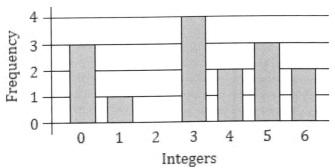

Integers

3. * The graph above shows the frequency distribution of a list of randomly generated integers between 0 and 6. What is the mean of the list of numbers?

4. A biologist was interested in the number of times a field cricket chirps each minute on a sunny day. He randomly selected 100 field crickets from a garden, and found that the mean number of chirps per minute was 112, and the margin of error for this estimate was 6 chirps. The biologist would like to repeat the procedure and attempt to reduce the margin of error. Which of the following samples would most likely result in a smaller margin of error for the estimated mean number of times a field cricket chirps each minute on a sunny day?

   (A) 50 randomly selected crickets from the same garden.
   (B) 50 randomly selected field crickets from the same garden.
   (C) 200 randomly selected crickets from the same garden.
   (D) 200 randomly selected field crickets from the same garden.

LEVEL 2: STATISTICS

5. The average (arithmetic mean) of five numbers is 73. If one of the numbers is 67, what is the sum of the other four?

6. * The average (arithmetic mean) of seven numbers is 26. If an eighth number, 14, is added to the group, what is the average of the eight numbers?

7. For which of the following lists of 6 numbers is the mode NOT equal to the average (arithmetic mean)?

   (A) 2, 3, 3, 3, 3, 4
   (B) 2, 4, 4, 4, 5, 5
   (C) 3, 3, 3, 3, 5, 6
   (D) 4, 4, 5, 5, 5, 7

LEVEL 3: STATISTICS

8. The average (arithmetic mean) of nine numbers is 30. When a tenth number is added, the average of the ten numbers is also 30. What is the tenth number?

9. The average of x, y, z, and w is 12 and the average of z and w is 7. What is the average of x and y?

10. The tables below give the distribution of the grades received by a class of 35 students on a math exam and a chemistry exam.

Math Exam			Chemistry Exam	
Grade	Frequency		Grade	Frequency
100	7		100	1
95	5		95	4
90	5		90	26
85	4		85	2
80	6		80	1
75	8		75	1

Which of the following is true about the data shown for these 35 students?

(A) The standard deviation of grades on the math exam is larger.

(B) The standard deviation of grades on the chemistry exam is larger.

(C) The standard deviation of grades on the math exam is the same as that of the chemistry exam.

(D) The standard deviation of grades on these two exams cannot be calculated with the data provided.

Answers

1. 144	6. 24.5
2. A	7. C
3. 16/5 or 3.2	8. 30
4. D	9. 17
5. 298	10. A

LESSON 21
COMPLEX NUMBERS

Reminder: Before beginning this lesson remember to redo the problems from Lessons 1, 5, 9, 13 and 17 that you have marked off. Do not "unmark" a question unless you get it correct.

Complex Numbers

A **complex number** has the form $a + bi$ where a and b are real numbers and $i = \sqrt{-1}$.

Example: The following are complex numbers:

$$2 + 3i \quad \frac{3}{2} + (-2i) = \frac{3}{2} - 2i \quad -\pi + 2.6i \quad \sqrt{-9} = 3i$$

$0 + 5i = 5i$ This is called a **pure imaginary** number.

$17 + 0i = 17$ This is called a **real number.**

$0 + 0i = 0$ This is **zero.**

Addition and subtraction: We add two complex numbers simply by adding their real parts, and then adding their imaginary parts.

$$(a + bi) + (c + di) = (a + c) + (b + d)i$$

LEVEL 1: COMPLEX NUMBERS

1. For $i = \sqrt{-1}$, the sum $(2 + 3i) + (5 - 7i)$ is

(A) $7 + 10i$
(B) $7 - 4i$
(C) $3 + 10i$
(D) $3 - 4i$

* $(2 + 3i) + (5 - 7i) = (2 + 5) + (3 - 7)i = 7 - 4i$, choice (B).

Multiplication: We can multiply two complex numbers by formally taking the product of two binomials and then replacing i^2 by -1.

$$(a + bi)(c + di) = (ac - bd) + (ad + bc)i$$

LEVEL 3: COMPLEX NUMBERS

2. Which of the following complex numbers is equivalent to $(1 + 2i)(3 - 4i)$? (Note: $i = \sqrt{-1}$)

    (A) $3 - 8i$
    (B) $4 - 2i$
    (C) $11 + 2i$
    (D) $11 - 2i$

* $(1 + 2i)(3 - 4i) = (3 + 8) + (-4 + 6)i = 11 + 2i$, choice (C).

The **conjugate** of the complex number $a + bi$ is the complex number $a - bi$.

Example: The conjugate of $-5 + 6i$ is $-5 - 6i$.

Note that when we multiply conjugates together we always get a real number. In fact, we have

$$(a + bi)(a - bi) = a^2 + b^2$$

Division: We can put the quotient of two complex numbers into standard form by multiplying both the numerator and denominator by the conjugate of the denominator. This is best understood with an example.

LEVEL 4: COMPLEX NUMBERS

$$\frac{1 + 5i}{2 - 3i}$$

3. If the expression above is rewritten in the form $a + bi$, where a and b are real numbers, what is the value of $b - a$?

* We multiply the numerator and denominator of $\frac{1+5i}{2-3i}$ by $(2 + 3i)$ to get

$$\frac{(1+5i)}{(2-3i)} \cdot \frac{(2+3i)}{(2+3i)} = \frac{(2-15)+(3+10)i}{4+9} = \frac{-13+13i}{13} = -\frac{13}{13} + \frac{13}{13}i = -1 + i$$

So $a = -1$, $b = 1$, and $b - a = 1 - (-1) = 1 + 1 = \mathbf{2}$.

Now try to solve each of the following problems. The answers to these problems, followed by full solutions are at the end of this lesson. **Do not** look at the answers until you have attempted these problems yourself. Please remember to mark off any problems you get wrong.

LEVEL 1: COMPLEX NUMBERS

4. If $(-5 + 2i) + (-1 - 3i) = a + bi$ and $i = \sqrt{-1}$, then what is the value of ab ?

LEVEL 2: COMPLEX NUMBERS

5. When we subtract $2 - 3i$ from $-5 + 6i$ we get which of the following complex numbers?

   (A) $-7 + 3i$
   (B) $-7 + 9i$
   (C) $-3 - 3i$
   (D) $-3 + 3i$

6. If $i = \sqrt{-1}$, and $(3 + 5i)(3 - 5i) = a + bi$, where a and b are real numbers, then what is the value of a?

Answers

1. B
2. C
3. 2

4. 6
5. B
6. 34

Full Solutions

4.
* $(-5 + 2i) + (-1 - 3i) = (-5 - 1) + (2 - 3)i = -6 - i$. So $a = -6$, $b = -1$, and therefore $ab = (-6)(-1) = $ **6**.

5.
* $(-5 + 6i) - (2 - 3i) = -5 + 6i - 2 + 3i = -7 + 9i$, choice (B).

6.
* $(3 + 5i)(3 - 5i) = 9 + 25 = 34 = 34 + 0i$. So $a = $ **34**.

LESSON 22
GEOMETRY

Reminder: Before beginning this lesson remember to redo the problems from Lessons 2, 6, 10, 14 and 18 that you have marked off. Do not "unmark" a question unless you get it correct.

Parallel Lines Cut by a Transversal

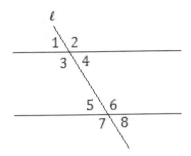

The figure above shows two parallel lines cut by the transversal ℓ.

Angles 1, 4, 5, and 8 all have the same measure. Also, angles 2, 3, 6, and 7 all have the same measure. Any two angles that do not have the same measure are supplementary, that is their measures add to 180°.

LEVEL 2: GEOMETRY

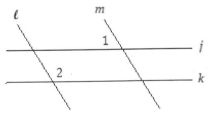

1. In the figure above, lines j and k are parallel and lines ℓ and m are parallel. If the measure of ∠1 is 68°, what is the measure of ∠2 ?

    (A) 158°
    (B) 112°
    (C) 98°
    (D) 68°

144

* $m\angle 2 = 180° - m\angle 1 = 180° - 68° = 112°$, choice (B).

Similarity

Two triangles are **similar** if their angles are congruent. Note that similar triangles **do not** have to be the same size. Also, note that to show that two triangles are similar we need only show that two pairs of angles are congruent. We get the third pair for free because all triangles have angle measures summing to 180 degrees.

Example:

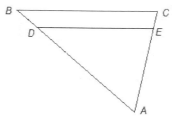

In the figure above, assume that $\overline{BC}$ is parallel to $\overline{DE}$. It then follows that angles ADE and ABC are congruent (corresponding angles). Since triangles ADE and ABC share angle A, the two triangles are similar.

Important Fact: Corresponding sides of similar triangles are in proportion.

So for example, in the figure above, $\dfrac{AD}{AB} = \dfrac{DE}{BC}$.

LEVEL 2: GEOMETRY

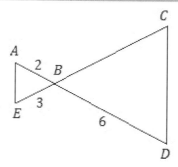

2.   In the figure above, $AE \parallel CD$ and segment AD intersects segment CE at B. What is the length of segment CE ?

* $\dfrac{BC}{BE} = \dfrac{BD}{BA}$. So $\dfrac{BC}{3} = \dfrac{6}{2}$. Thus, $2BC = 18$, and so $BC = \dfrac{18}{2} = 9$.

It follows that $CE = BC + BE = 9 + 3 = \mathbf{12}$.

You're doing great! Let's just practice a bit more. Try to solve each of the following problems by using one of the strategies you just learned. Then, if possible, solve each problem another way. The answers to these problems, followed by full solutions are at the end of this lesson. **Do not** look at the answers until you have attempted these problems yourself. Please remember to mark off any problems you get wrong.

LEVEL 2: GEOMETRY

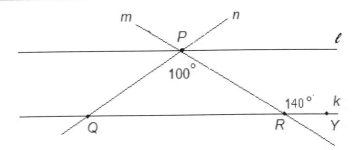

3.   In the figure above, line ℓ is parallel to line k. Transversals m and n intersect at point P on ℓ and intersect k at points R and Q, respectively. Point Y is on k, the measure of $\angle PRY$ is 140°, and the measure of $\angle QPR$ is 100°. How many of the angles formed by rays ℓ, k, m, and n have measure 40° ?

   (A) 4
   (B) 6
   (C) 8
   (D) 10

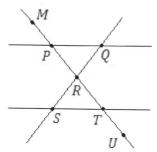

Note: Figure not drawn to scale.

4.   In the figure above, $\angle MPQ \cong \angle STU$. Each of the following statements must be true EXCEPT

   (A) $\overline{PQ} \parallel \overline{ST}$
   (B) $m\angle MPQ + m\angle RTS = 180°$
   (C) $\Delta PQR \sim \Delta TSR$
   (D) $\Delta PQR \cong \Delta TSR$

LEVEL 3: GEOMETRY

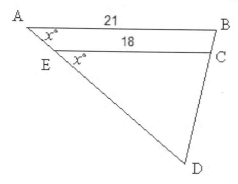

5.   In the figure above, what is the value of $\frac{ED}{AD}$?

   (A) $\frac{1}{7}$

   (B) $\frac{1}{4}$

   (C) $\frac{1}{2}$

   (D) $\frac{6}{7}$

147

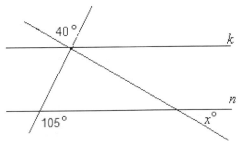

Note: Figure not drawn to scale.

6.   In the figure above, $k \parallel n$. What is the value of x?

Answers

1. B	4. D
2. 12	5. D
3. C	6. 65

Full Solutions

3.

* $\angle QRP$ is supplementary with $\angle PRY$. So $m\angle QRP$ is $180 - 140 = 40°$. We can then use vertical angles to get the remaining angles in the lower right hand corner.

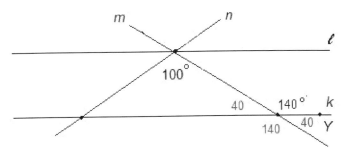

We now use the fact that the sum of the angle measures in a triangle is 180° to get that the measure of the third angle of the triangle is $180 - 100 - 40 = 40°$. We then once again use supplementary and vertical angles to get the remaining angles in the lower left hand corner.

148

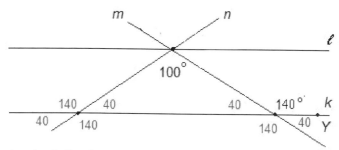

Now notice the following alternate interior angles.

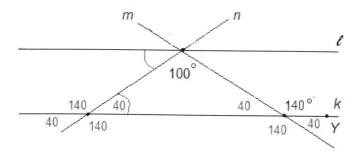

Since $\ell \parallel k$, the alternate interior angles are congruent. So, the angle marked above has a measure of 40°. We use supplementary and vertical angles to find the remaining angle measures.

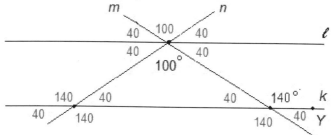

Finally, we see that there are eight angles with measure 40°, choice (C).

4.

* Solution by drawing another representation of the figure: Since the figure is not drawn to scale, let's draw a second representation of the figure, different from the given one, that satisfies the given condition.

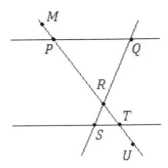

Note that we drew the figure so that $\angle MPQ \cong \angle STU$ is still true. Since $\triangle PQR$ is clearly larger than $\triangle TSR$, we see that $\triangle PQR \cong \triangle TSR$ can be false, choice (D).

Notes: (1) The symbol $\|$ stands for "parallel," so that $\overline{PQ} \parallel \overline{ST}$ is read "segment PQ is parallel to segment ST."

(2) $m\angle MPQ$ is read "the measure of angle MPQ." So, choice (B) can be read "the sum of the measures of angle MPQ and angle RTS is 180 degrees."

(3) The symbol $\sim$ stands for "similar," so that $\triangle PQR \sim \triangle TSR$ is read "triangle PQR is similar to triangle TSR."

Two triangles are **similar** if they have the same angle measures.

(4) In this problem, $\angle PRQ$ and $\angle TRS$ are **vertical angles**. Since vertical angles have the same measure, $m\angle PRQ = m\angle TRS$.

It is also true that $m\angle PQR = m\angle TSR$ and $m\angle QPR = m\angle STR$. See the next solution for details.

It follows that $\triangle PQR \sim \triangle TSR$.

(5) To determine that two triangles are similar, it is sufficient to show that two pairs of angles have the same measure. We get the third pair for free because the angle measures in a triangle always sum to $180°$.

(6) The symbol $\cong$ stands for "congruent," so that $\angle MPQ \cong \angle STU$ is read "angle MPQ is congruent to angle STU," and $\triangle PQR \cong \triangle TSR$ is read "triangle PQR is congruent to triangle TSR."

Two line segments are **congruent** if they have the same length. Two angles are **congruent** if they have the same measure. Two triangles are **congruent** if all corresponding sides and interior angles are congruent.

In the last figure we drew, we have $\angle PRQ \cong \angle TRS$ (because they are vertical angles), but $\triangle PQR \not\cong \triangle TSR$.

* **Solution by process of elimination:** Let's first redraw the picture with just one transversal.

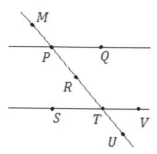

So, we have the lines $\overline{PQ}$ and $\overline{ST}$ cut by the transversal $\overline{MU}$ with $\angle MPQ \cong \angle STU$. By the converse to the alternate exterior angle theorem, we have $\overline{PQ} \parallel \overline{ST}$. So, we can eliminate choice (A).

It then follows that the parallel lines and transversal form 8 angles, any two of which are congruent or supplementary. Since angles MPQ and RTS are clearly not necessarily congruent (in the above figure one is obtuse, the other acute), they must be supplementary. It follows that $m\angle MPQ + m\angle RTS = 180°$, and so we can eliminate choice (B).

Now since $\overline{PQ} \parallel \overline{ST}$, it follows that the alternate interior angles cut by the transversal are congruent. That is $\angle QPR \cong \angle STR$. In the original figure, we also have $\angle PRQ \cong \angle TRS$ because vertical angles are congruent. It follows that $\triangle PQR \sim \triangle TSR$, and so we can eliminate choice (C).

Since we have eliminated choices (A), (B), and (C), the answer is (D).

Notes: (1) In the last figure above with lines $\overline{PQ}$ and $\overline{ST}$ cut by the transversal $\overline{MU}$, we have the following definitions:

    (a) $\angle MPQ$ and $\angle STU$ are called **alternate exterior angles**.
    (b) $\angle QPR$ and $\angle STR$ are called **alternate interior angles**.
    (c) $\angle MPQ$ and $\angle RTV$ are called **corresponding angles**.

Observe that there is 1 more pair of alternate exterior angles, 1 more pair of alternate interior angles, and 3 more pairs of corresponding angles. Can you find them?

(2) If the lines $\overline{PQ}$ and $\overline{ST}$ happen to be parallel, then the alternate exterior angles formed are congruent. This is known as the **alternate exterior angle theorem**.

(3) There are also two similar theorems for alternate interior angles and corresponding angles.

(4) The converses of each of these theorems are also true. For example, the converse to the alternate exterior angle theorem says "If two lines are cut by a transversal and the alternate exterior angles formed are congruent, then the two lines are parallel.

Can you state the converses to the other two analogous theorems?

(5) To summarize the three main theorems, whenever parallel lines are cut by a transversal, eight angles are formed.

We can split these eight angles into two groups of four. Any two angles in each group are congruent, and if we take two angles from different groups they are supplementary (their measures add to $180°$).

For example, $\angle MPQ \cong \angle STU$, whereas $m\angle MPQ + m\angle RTS = 180°$.

(6) Many of the notes from the first solution to this problem are relevant for this solution as well.

    5.

* **Solution by assuming the figure is drawn to scale:** (This solution was also done in Lesson 10) Clearly ED is more than half the size of AD, so that $\frac{ED}{AD} > \frac{1}{2}$. Thus, the answer is $\frac{6}{7}$, choice (D).

Geometric solution: Triangles ECD and ABD are **similar**, and **corresponding sides of similar triangles are in proportion**. Therefore

$$\frac{ED}{AD} = \frac{EC}{AB} = \frac{18}{21} = \frac{6}{7}$$

Thus, the answer is choice (D).

Remarks: (1) To see that triangles ABD and ECD are similar, observe that BAD and CED are congruent, and the two triangles share angle D.

(2) When a triangle is inside another similar triangle it may help to draw the individual triangles next to each other, oriented so that congruent angles are in the same direction. See the figures below.

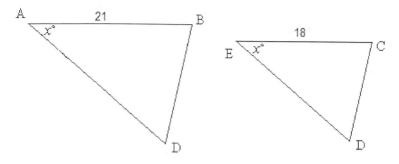

6.

* We will use supplementary angles, vertical angles, and the fact that the angle measures of a triangle sum to $180°$ to find x.

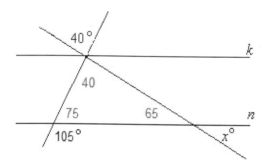

To clarify the picture above, $180 - 105 = 75$, the upper angle of the triangle has measure $40°$ because it is vertical with the other $40°$ angle, and $180 - 75 - 40 = 65$. Since the angle labeled by x is vertical with the 65 degree angle, $x = \mathbf{65}$.

LESSON 23
PASSPORT TO ADVANCED MATH

Reminder: Before beginning this lesson remember to redo the problems from Lessons 3, 7, 11, 15 and 19 that you have marked off. Do not "unmark" a question unless you get it correct.

Square Root Property

The **square root property** says that if $x^2 = a^2$, then $x = \pm a$.

For example, the equation $x^2 = 9$ has the two solutions $x = 3$ and $x = -3$.

Important note: Using the square root property is different from taking a square root. We apply the square root property to an equation of the form $x^2 = a^2$ to get two solutions, whereas when we take the positive square root of a number we get just one answer.

For example, when we take the positive square root of 9 we get 3, i.e. $\sqrt{9} = 3$. But when we apply the square root property to the equation $x^2 = 9$, we have seen that we get the two solutions $x = 3$ and $x = -3$.

LEVEL 3: ADVANCED MATH

$$(x - 3)^2 = 2$$

1.   What is the solution set of the above equation?

  (A) $\{1, 5\}$
  (B) $\{3 + \sqrt{2}\}$
  (C) $\{3 - \sqrt{2}, 3 + \sqrt{2}\}$
  (D) The equation has no solutions.

* Solution using the square root property: When we apply the square root property we get $x - 3 = \pm\sqrt{2}$. We then add 3 to each side of this last equation to get the two solutions $x = 3 \pm \sqrt{2}$, choice (C).

Solving Quadratic Equations

A quadratic equation has the form $ax^2 + bx + c = 0$.

Let's use a simple example to illustrate the various methods for solving such an equation

LEVEL 3: ADVANCED MATH

$$x^2 - 2x = 15$$

2.   In the quadratic equation above, find the positive solution for x.

Solution by guessing: We plug in guesses for x until we find the answer. For example, if we guess that $x = 3$, we get $3^2 - 2 \cdot 3 = 9 - 6 = 3$. This is too small.

Let's try $x = 5$ next. We get $5^2 - 2 \cdot 5 = 25 - 10 = 15$. This is correct. So, the answer is **5**.

Solution by factoring: We bring everything to the left-hand side of the equation to get $x^2 - 2x - 15 = 0$. We then factor the left-hand side to get $(x - 5)(x + 3) = 0$. So $x - 5 = 0$ or $x + 3 = 0$. It follows that $x = 5$ or $x = -3$. Since we want the positive solution for x, the answer is **5**.

Solution by using the quadratic formula: As in the last solution we bring everything to the left-hand side of the equation to get

$$x^2 - 2x - 15 = 0.$$

We identify $a = 1$, $b = -2$, and $c = -15$.

$$x = \frac{-b \pm \sqrt{b^2 - 4ac}}{2a} = \frac{2 \pm \sqrt{4 + 60}}{2} = \frac{2 \pm \sqrt{64}}{2} = \frac{2 \pm 8}{2} = \mathbf{1 \pm 4.}$$

So we get $x = 1 + 4 = 5$ or $x = 1 - 4 = -3$. Since we want the positive solution for x, the answer is **5**.

Graphical solution: In your graphing calculator press the Y= button, and enter the following.

$$Y1 = X^2 - 2X - 15$$

Now press ZOOM 6 to graph the parabola in a standard window. Then press 2nd TRACE (which is CALC) 2 (or select ZERO), move the cursor just to the left of the second x-intercept and press ENTER. Now move the cursor just to the right of the second x-intercept and press ENTER again. Press ENTER once more, and you will see that the x-coordinate of the second x-intercept is **5**.

Sum and Product of Roots of a Quadratic Function

Let r and s be the roots of the quadratic equation $x^2 + bx + c = 0$. Then

$$b = -(r + s) \quad \text{and} \quad c = rs.$$

Try to answer the following question using one of these formulas. **Do not** check the solution until you have attempted this question yourself.

LEVEL 4: ADVANCED MATH

3. What is the sum of all values of k that satisfy $k^2 - 13k + 7 = 0$?

* We are being asked to find the sum of the roots of the quadratic equation. This is **13**.

Notes: (1) The sum of the roots of a quadratic equation of the form $x^2 + bx + c = 0$ is simply $-b$. In words, the sum of the roots is simply the negative of the coefficient of x.

In this problem, the variable is k so that the sum of the roots is simply the negative of the coefficient of k. This is $-(-13) = 13$.

(2) If we let r and s be the roots of the given quadratic equation, then using the formula above we have that $-13 = -(r + s)$ so that $13 = r + s$. That is the sum of the roots is 13.

Now try to solve each of the following problems. The answers to these problems, followed by full solutions are at the end of this lesson. **Do not** look at the answers until you have attempted these problems yourself. Please remember to mark off any problems you get wrong.

LEVEL 3: ADVANCED MATH

4. In the xy-plane, the parabola with equation $y = (x - 3)^2$ intersects the line with equation $y = 4$ at two points, P and Q. What is the length of $\overline{PQ}$?

LEVEL 4: ADVANCED MATH

5.   What are the solutions to $x^2 - 6x + 4 = 0$?

   (A) $x = -20 \pm 20\sqrt{5}$
   (B) $x = -20 \pm \sqrt{5}$
   (C) $x = 3 \pm 20\sqrt{5}$
   (D) $x = 3 \pm \sqrt{5}$

$$(x - n)(x - 9) = x^2 - 4nx + k$$

6.   In the equation above, n and k are constants. If the equation is true for all values of x, what is the value of k ?

Answers

1. C	4. 4
2. 5	5. D
3. 13	6. 27

Full Solutions

4.

* **Solution using the square root property:** Replacing y with 4 in the first equation yields $(x - 3)^2 = 4$. We use the square root property to get $x - 3 = \pm 2$. So $x = 3 \pm 2$. So, the two solutions are $x = 3 + 2 = 5$ and $x = 3 - 2 = 1$.

So $P = (1,4)$ and $Q = (5,4)$. The distance between these two points is $|5 - 1| = |4| = $ **4**.

Notes: (1) To find the points of intersection of the parabola and the line, we solved the given system of equations. We chose to use the **substitution method** here.

(2) Instead of formally applying the square root property to solve $(x - 3)^2 = 4$, we can simply "guess" the solutions, or solve the equation informally. It's not too hard to see that $x = 1$ and $x = 5$ will make the equation true.

(3) It's not necessary to write down the points P and Q. Since the y-coordinates of the two points are the same, we can simply subtract one x-value from the other (disregarding the minus sign if it appears) to get the desired distance.

(4) We can also plot the two points and observe that the distance between them is 4.

5.

* Let's solve this equation using the quadratic formula. We identify $a = 1, b = -6$, and $c = 4$.

$$x = \frac{-b \pm \sqrt{b^2 - 4ac}}{2a} = \frac{6 \pm \sqrt{36 - 16}}{2} = \frac{6 \pm \sqrt{20}}{2} = \frac{6 \pm 2\sqrt{5}}{2} = 3 \pm \sqrt{5}.$$

This is choice (D).

Notes: (1) $\sqrt{20} = \sqrt{4 \cdot 5} = \sqrt{4} \cdot \sqrt{5} = 2\sqrt{5}$

(2) $\frac{6 \pm 2\sqrt{5}}{2} = \frac{6}{2} \pm \frac{2\sqrt{5}}{2} = 3 \pm \sqrt{5}$

6.

* The left-hand side is 0 when $x = 9$ and $x = n$. The coefficient of x is the negative of the sum of these roots, and so $4n = n + 9$, or $3n = 9$. So $n = 3$. The constant term is the product of these roots, so that $k = 9 \cdot 3 = \mathbf{27}$.

Download additional solutions for free here:

www.thesatmathprep.com/28Les400.html

LESSON 24
PROBLEM SOLVING

Reminder: Before beginning this lesson remember to redo the problems from Lessons 4, 8, 12, 16, and 20 that you have marked off. Do not "unmark" a question unless you get it correct.

Try to solve each of the following problems. The answers to these problems, followed by full solutions are at the end of this lesson. **Do not** look at the answers until you have attempted these problems yourself. Please remember to mark off any problems you get wrong.

LEVEL 1: PROBLEM SOLVING

1. If x hours and 17 minutes is equal to 677 minutes, what is the value of x ?

2. * A 770-gallon tank is filled to capacity with water. At most how many 14 ounce bottles can be filled with water from the tank? (1 gallon = 128 ounces)

LEVEL 2: PROBLEM SOLVING

3. * A chemist has a supply of 5.2 liter bottles of a certain solvent that must be shipped to a central warehouse. The warehouse can accept the solvent at the rate of 3 hectoliters per minute for a maximum of 8 hours per day. If 1 hectoliter equals 100 liters, what is the maximum number of bottles that the warehouse could receive from the chemist each day?

    (A) 461
    (B) 462
    (C) 27,692
    (D) 83,200

159

LEVEL 3: PROBLEM SOLVING

4. A certain exam lasts a total of 4 hours. Each part of the exam requires the same amount of time and 10 minute breaks are included between consecutive parts. If there is a total of 4 breaks during the 4 hours, what is the required time, in minutes, for each part of the test?

5. A bus driver drove at an average speed of 45 miles per hour for 3 hours while the bus consumed fuel at a rate of 15 miles per gallon. How many gallons of fuel did the bus use for the entire 3-hour trip?

6. * John, a United States resident, is on vacation in Spain and uses his credit card to purchase a souvenir for 184 euros. The bank that issues the credit card converts the purchase price at the foreign exchange rate for that day, and an additional fee of 6% of the converted cost is applied before the bank posts the charge. If the bank posts a charge of $212 to John's account, what exchange rate, in Euros per one U.S. dollar, did the bank use?

Answers

1. 11
2. 7040
3. C

4. 40
5. 9
6. .92

Full Solutions

1.
Since there are 60 minutes in an hour we note that $60 \cdot 11 = 660$. So 660 minutes is 11 hours. Since $677 - 660 = 17$, we see that 677 minutes is 11 hours and 17 minutes. Thus, the answer is **11**.

* **Quick solution:** $677 - 17 = 660$ and $\frac{660}{60} = \mathbf{11}$.

2.
* 770 gallons is equal to $770 \cdot 128 = 98,560$ ounces. Therefore, the number of bottles that can be filled is $\frac{98,560}{14} = \mathbf{7040}$.

Notes: (1) Since there are 128 ounces in a gallon, 770 gallons is the same as $770 \cdot 128 = 98,560$ ounces.

(2) We can convert between gallons and ounces more formally by setting up a ratio.

$$
\begin{array}{ccc}
\text{gallons} & 770 & 1 \\
\text{ounces} & x & 128
\end{array}
$$

Now draw in the division symbols and equal sign, cross multiply and divide the corresponding ratio to find the unknown quantity x.

$$\frac{770}{x} = \frac{1}{128}$$

$$1x = 770 \cdot 128$$

$$x = 98{,}560$$

(3) Instead of converting 770 gallons to 98,560 ounces, and then dividing by 14, we can instead convert 14 ounces to $\frac{14}{128} = .109375$ gallons, and then divide $\frac{770}{.109375} = 7040$.

    3.

* The warehouse can receive $3 \cdot 60 \cdot 8 = 1440$ hectoliters of the solvent per day, or equivalently, $1440 \cdot 100 = 144{,}000$ liters of the solvent per day. Therefore, the number of bottles that can be accepted each day is $\frac{144{,}000}{5.2} \approx 27{,}692.30769$. The maximum number of bottles that the warehouse can accept in one day is therefore 27,692, choice (C).

Notes: (1) Since there are 60 minutes in an hour, "3 hectoliters per minute" is the same as $3 \cdot 60 = 180$ hectoliters per hour.

Similarly, since the warehouse can accept the solvent for a maximum of 8 hours per day, "180 hectoliters per hour" is equivalent to a maximum of $180 \cdot 8 = 1440$ hectoliters per day.

(2) In the above solution we combined the two conversions given in note (1) into a single conversion: "3 hectoliters per minute" is equivalent to a maximum of $3 \cdot 60 \cdot 8 = 1440$ hectoliters per day.

(3) Since 1 hectoliter equals 100 liters, we can convert hectoliters to liters by multiplying by 100. So

    1440 hectoliters is equal to $1440 \cdot 100 = 144{,}000$ liters.

(4) We can convert between hectoliters and liters more formally by setting up a ratio. The two things being compared are "liters" and "hectoliters."

liters	100	x
hectoliters	1	1440

Now draw in the division symbols and equal sign, cross multiply and divide the corresponding ratio to find the unknown quantity x.

$$\frac{100}{1} = \frac{x}{1440}$$

$$1x = 100 \cdot 1440$$

$$x = 144{,}000$$

(5) Instead of converting 1440 hectoliters to 144,000 liters, and then dividing by 5.2, we can instead convert 5.2 liters to $\frac{5.2}{100} = .052$ hectoliters, and then divide $\frac{1440}{.052} \approx 27{,}692.30769$, giving the same answer of 27,692, choice (C).

4.

* The exam lasts $4(60) = 240$ minutes. There is a total of $4(10) = 40$ minutes in breaks. So, each part of the test lasts $\frac{200}{5} = \mathbf{40}$ minutes.

Note: Since there are 4 breaks, there must be 5 parts to the exam (breaks fall between consecutive parts). A common error is to mistakenly assume that there are only 4 parts to the exam.

5.

* The bus driver drove $d = r \cdot t = 45 \cdot 3 = 135$ miles, and so the amount of fuel that the bus used was $\frac{135}{15} = \mathbf{9}$ gallons.

Notes: (1) We used the formula "distance = rate × time" or $d = r \cdot t$.

In this problem, the rate is $r = 45$ miles/hour and the time is $t = 3$ hours.

(2) The bus gets 15 miles for each gallon of fuel. So, the bus can drive 15 miles on one gallon of fuel. The bus can drive $15 \cdot 2 = 30$ miles on two gallons of fuel. The bus can drive $15 \cdot 3 = 45$ miles on three gallons of fuel. And so on.

In general, the bus can drive $15x$ miles on x gallons of fuel.

So, we have $15x = 135$, where x is the number of gallons of fuel needed to travel 135 miles. So $x = \frac{135}{15} = 9$.

6.

* If we let C be the original cost of the item in dollars, then we have $C + .06C = 212$, or equivalently $1.06C = 212$. So $C = \frac{212}{1.06} = 200$.

So, we know that 184 euros corresponds to 200 dollars. We want to know how many euros correspond to 1 dollar. So, we set up a ratio.

The two things being compared are "euros" and "dollars."

$$
\begin{array}{ccc}
\text{euros} & 184 & x \\
\text{dollars} & 200 & 1
\end{array}
$$

Now draw in the division symbols and equal sign, cross multiply and divide the corresponding ratio to find the unknown quantity x.

$$\frac{184}{200} = \frac{x}{1}$$

$$200x = 184 \cdot 1$$

$$x = \frac{184}{200} = .92$$

So we grid in $.\mathbf{92}$.

LESSON 25
HEART OF ALGEBRA

Try to solve each of the following problems. The answers to these problems are at the end of this lesson.

Full solutions to these problems are available for free download here:

www.thesatmathprep.com/28Les400.html

LEVEL 1: HEART OF ALGEBRA

$$\frac{3 + \omega}{2} = 3\frac{1}{2}$$

1. What number, when used in place of ω above, makes the statement true?

   (A) 4
   (B) 5
   (C) 10
   (D) 12

2. If $10 + x = 5 + x + x$, what is the value of x ?

   (A) 5
   (B) 4
   (C) 3
   (D) 2

3. If $8c + 1 < 25$, which of the following CANNOT be the value of C ?

   (A) 0
   (B) 1
   (C) 2
   (D) 3

4. If $b = a - 2$, and $11b - 4b = 28$ what is the value of a?

   (A) 2
   (B) 4
   (C) 6
   (D) 8

164

5. If $j > 0$, for what value of j will $j^2 - 3 = 33$?

6. If $3^4 = 9^z$, then $z =$

    (A) 4
    (B) 3
    (C) 2
    (D) 1

7. Which of the following expressions is equivalent to 9 less than the product of c and d?

    (A) $c + d - 9$
    (B) $cd - 9$
    (C) $9cd$
    (D) $9(c - d)$

8. Megan is selling $5d$ bracelets at a price of p dollars each. If x is the number of bracelets she did <u>not</u> sell, which of the following represents the total dollar amount she received in sales from the bracelets?

    (A) $px - 5d$
    (B) $5d - px$
    (C) $p(x - 5d)$
    (D) $p(5d - x)$

9. James solved k math problems per hour for 3 hours and Paul solved t math problems per hour for 2 hours. Which of the following represents the total number of math problems solved by James and Paul?

    (A) $2k + 3t$
    (B) $3k + 2t$
    (C) $6kt$
    (D) $5kt$

10. If $4y - 32 = 20$, then $y - 8 =$

    (A) 20
    (B) 15
    (C) 10
    (D) 5

165

11. If $i = \sqrt{-1}$, then $(3 - 2i) + (-1 + 3i) =$

    (A) $2 - i$
    (B) $2 + i$
    (C) $4 - i$
    (D) $4 - 5i$

LEVEL 2: HEART OF ALGEBRA

12. If $(x - 2)^2 = 16$, and $x < 0$, what is the value of x ?

    (A) -9
    (B) -3
    (C) -2
    (D) -1

13. If $|3 - 8x| > 34$, which of the following is a possible value of x?

    (A) -4
    (B) -2
    (C) $\;\;2$
    (D) $\;\;4$

14. If $\frac{a}{b} = -5$, then $a + 5b =$

    (A) 0
    (B) 1
    (C) a
    (D) b

15. If $4^{x+3} = 4096$, what is the value of x ?

16. If $5x + 11 = 43$, then $5x - 11 =$

$$6 - 2c \geq 7 - 2c$$

17. Which of the following best describes the solutions to the inequality above?

    (A) $c \leq 1$
    (B) $c \geq 1$
    (C) All real numbers
    (D) No solution

18. What number increased by 12 equals 5 times the number?

19. * Gina subscribes to a cell phone service that charges a monthly fee of $60.00. The first 500 megabytes of data is free, and the cost is $0.15 for each additional megabyte of data used that month. Which of the following functions gives the cost, in dollars, for a month in which Gina uses x megabytes of data, where $x > 500$.

    (A) $60 + 15x$
    (B) $0.15x - 15$
    (C) $0.15x - 440$
    (D) $60 + 0.15x$

20. If $x + 5y = 13$ and $x + 11y = 9$, what is the value of $x + 8y$?

21. If $\frac{a+5}{3} = 10$ and $\frac{a+b}{8} = 12$, what is the value of b?

LEVEL 3: HEART OF ALGEBRA

22. If $5^x = 7$, then $5^{2x} =$

    (A) 11
    (B) 13
    (C) 25
    (D) 49

23. If x is $\frac{2}{7}$ of y and y is $\frac{7}{8}$ of z, what is the value of $\frac{z}{x}$?

    (A) $\frac{1}{4}$

    (B) $\frac{3}{4}$

    (C) 1

    (D) 4

24. If $\frac{a}{b} = \frac{10}{c}$, which of the following must equal 10?

    (A) a
    (B) b
    (C) c
    (D) $\frac{ac}{b}$

167

25. What is one possible value of x for which $x < 3 < \frac{1}{x}$?

$$T = 25 + 3c$$

26. The equation above is used to model the number of chirps, c, made by a certain species of cricket in one minute, and the temperature, T, in degrees Fahrenheit. According to this model, what is the estimated increase in temperature, in degrees Fahrenheit, when the number of chirps in one minute is increased by 1?

  (A) 3
  (B) 5
  (C) 25
  (D) 28

27. If $20x + 24y = 40$, what is the value of $5x + 6y$?

$$
\begin{array}{cc}
7m & 3m \\
9 & 9 \\
2k & j \\
3 & 3 \\
+5 & +5 \\
\hline
26 & 12
\end{array}
$$

28. In the correctly worked addition problems above, what is the value of $4m + 2k - j$?

29. If $i = \sqrt{-1}$, and $\frac{(3-2i)}{(-1+3i)} = a + bi$, where a and b are real numbers, then what is the value of $|a + b|$?

LEVEL 4: HEART OF ALGEBRA

30. Which of the following expressions is equal to -2 for some value of a?

  (A) $|a - 1| - 1$
  (B) $|1 - a| - 1$
  (C) $|a + 1| - 1$
  (D) $|a - 1| - 2$

168

31. If $y = 3^x$, which of the following expressions is equivalent to $9^x - 3^{x+2}$ for all positive integer values of x ?

   (A) y^2
   (B) $y^2 - y$
   (C) $y^2 - 3y$
   (D) $y^2 - 9y$

32. A small hotel has 15 rooms which are all occupied. If each room is occupied by either one or two guests and there are 27 guests in total, how many rooms are occupied by two guests?

Answers

1. A	9. B	17. D	25. $0 < x \leq .333$
2. A	10. D	18. 3	26. A
3. D	11. B	19. B	27. 10
4. C	12. C	20. 11	28. 14
5. 6	13. A	21. 71	29. 8/5 or 1.6
6. C	14. A	22. D	30. D
7. B	15. 3	23. D	31. D
8. D	16. 21	24. D	32. 12

LESSON 26
GEOMETRY AND TRIGONOMETRY

Try to solve each of the following problems. The answers to these problems are at the end of this lesson.

Full solutions to these problems are available for free download here:

www.thesatmathprep.com/28Les400.html

LEVEL 1: GEOMETRY AND TRIG

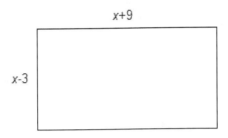

1. If the perimeter of the rectangle above is 80, what is the value of x?

    (A) 20
    (B) 19
    (C) 18
    (D) 17

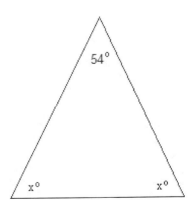

2. In the triangle above, what is the value of x ?

170

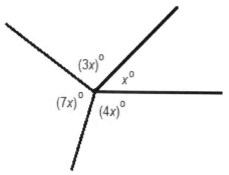

Note: Figure not drawn to scale.

3. In the figure above, four line segments meet at a point to form four angles. What is the value of x?

(A) 18
(B) 24
(C) 30
(D) 40

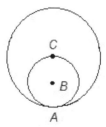

4. In the figure above, A, B, and C lie on the same line. B is the center of the smaller circle, and C is the center of the larger circle. If the radius of the smaller circle is 5, what is the diameter of the larger circle?

5. If the degree measures of the three angles of a triangle are $k°$, $k°$, and $85°$, what is the value of k?

6. What is the radius of a circle whose circumference is 7π?

7. In the standard (x, y) coordinate plane, what is the slope of the line segment joining the points $(3, -5)$ and $(7, 2)$?

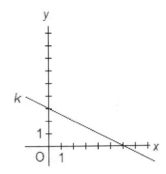

8. What is the equation of line k in the figure above?

    (A) $y = -2x + 3$

    (B) $y = -2x + 6$

    (C) $y = -\frac{1}{2}x + 3$

    (D) $y = -\frac{1}{2}x + 6$

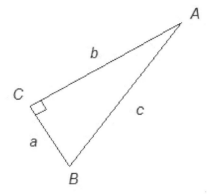

9. In the figure above, what is tan B ?

    (A) $\frac{c}{b}$

    (B) $\frac{a}{b}$

    (C) $\frac{a}{c}$

    (D) $\frac{b}{a}$

LEVEL 2: GEOMETRY

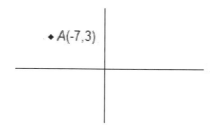

10. In the figure above, a line is to be drawn through point A so that it never crosses the y-axis. Through which of the following points must the line pass?

    (A) $(7, 3)$
    (B) $(7, -3)$
    (C) $(-7, -3)$
    (D) $(3, 7)$

11. What is the area of a right triangle whose sides have lengths 6, 8, and 10?

12. A line in the xy-plane passes through the origin and has a slope of $-\frac{2}{3}$. Which of the following points lies on the line?

    (A) $(-6, 4)$
    (B) $(3, -3)$
    (C) $(3, 2)$
    (D) $(0, \frac{2}{3})$

13. In the xy-plane, the point $(0, 3)$ is the center of a circle that has radius 3. Which of the following is NOT a point on the circle?

    (A) $(0, 6)$
    (B) $(-3, 6)$
    (C) $(3, 3)$
    (D) $(-3, 3)$

14. The sum of 7 adjacent nonoverlapping angles is 180 degrees. Six of the angles each have a measure of y degrees and the remaining angle measures 150 degrees. What is the value of y?

LEVEL 3: GEOMETRY AND TRIG

15. * The volume of a right circular cylinder is 3375π cubic centimeters. If the height and base radius of the cylinder are equal, what is the base radius of the cylinder?

   (A) 3 centimeters
   (B) 5 centimeters
   (C) 7 centimeters
   (D) 15 centimeters

16. Which of the following equations represents a line that is perpendicular to the line with equation $y = -2x - 3$?

   (A) $2x + 3y = 1$
   (B) $2x + y = 1$
   (C) $4x - 8y = 1$
   (D) $6x - 3y = 1$

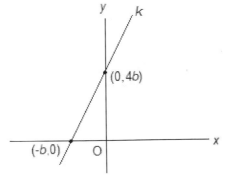

17. In the figure above, what is the slope of line k ?

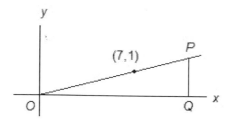

18. Line k (not shown) passes through O and intersects PQ between P and Q. What is one possible value of the slope of line k?

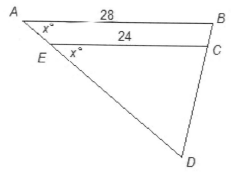

19. In the figure above, what is the value of $\frac{ED}{AD}$?

(A) $\frac{1}{7}$

(B) $\frac{2}{5}$

(C) $\frac{1}{2}$

(D) $\frac{6}{7}$

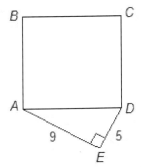

20. In the figure above, what is the area of square *ABCD* ?

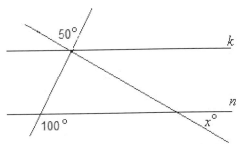

Note: Figure not drawn to scale.

21. In the figure above, $k \parallel n$. What is the value of x?

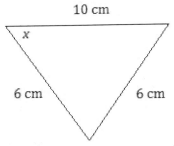

Note: Figure not drawn to scale.

22. The dimensions of a triangular block are shown above. What is the value of $\cos x$?

LEVEL 4: GEOMETRY

23. Point A is a vertex of an 8-sided polygon. The polygon has 8 sides of equal length and 8 angles of equal measure. When all possible diagonals are drawn from point A in the polygon, how many triangles are formed?

   (A) Two
   (B) Four
   (C) Six
   (D) Eight

24. Line k contains the point (4,0) and has slope 5. Which of the following points is on line k?

   (A) (1, 5)
   (B) (3, 5)
   (C) (5, 5)
   (D) (7, 5)

Answers

1. D	9. D	17. 4
2. 63	10. C	18. $0 < m < .143$
3. B	11. 24	19. D
4. 20	12. A	20. 106
5. 95/2 or 47.5	13. B	21. 50
6. 7/2 or 3.5	14. 5	22. 5/6 or .833
7. 7/4 or 1.75	15. D	23. C
8. C	16. C	24. C

LESSON 27
PASSPORT TO ADVANCED MATH

Try to solve each of the following problems. The answers to these problems are at the end of this lesson.

Full solutions to these problems are available for free download here:

www.thesatmathprep.com/28Les400.html

LEVEL 1: ADVANCED MATH

1. For the function $f(x) = 7x^2 + 3x$, what is the value of $f(-1)$?

2. If $14xz - 21yz = kz(2x - cy)$ where k and c are positive real numbers, what is the value of $k + c$?

LEVEL 2: ADVANCED MATH

$$f(x) = x^2 + 1$$
$$g(x) = 3 - 2x$$

3. The functions f and g are defined above. What is the value of $f(5) - g(6)$?

4. Let a function of 2 variables be defined by $g(x, y) = xy + 3xy^2 - (x - y^2)$. What is the value of $g(2, -1)$?

5. If $g(x) = -3x - 7$, what is $g(-4x)$ equal to?

    (A) $12x^2 + 28x$
    (B) $12x + 7$
    (C) $12x - 7$
    (D) $-12x + 7$

6. If $g(x - 3) = 5x + 1$ for all values of x, what is the value of $g(-2)$?

$$f(x) = |2x - 3| - 1$$

7. For what positive value of x is $f(x)$ equal to 2 ?

   (A) 0
   (B) 2
   (C) 3
   (D) There is no such positive value of x.

$$2(x - 3)(2x + 1)$$

8. If we rewrite the expression above in the form $ax^2 + bx + c$, then what is the value of $a - b$?

$$2x^2 - x - 4$$
$$3x^2 + 2x + 1$$

9. If the sum of the two polynomials given above is written in the form $ax^2 + bx + c$, then $a + b + c =$

LEVEL 3: ADVANCED MATH

10. Let h be a function such that $h(x) = |5x| + c$ where c is a constant. If $h(3) = -4$, what is the value of $h(-6)$?

11. Let the function g be defined for $x \neq 0$ by $g(x) = \dfrac{k}{x}$, where k is a constant. If $g(4) = 7$, what is $g(7)$?

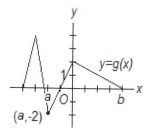

12. The figure above shows the graph of the function g in the xy-plane. For how many values of x between -4 and 4 does $g(x) = 3$?

13. The function p is defined by $p(x) = 5x^2 - cx + 8$, where c is a constant. In the xy-plane, the graph of $y = p(x)$ crosses the x-axis where $x = 4$. What is the value of c?

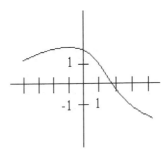

14. The figure above shows the graph of the function g. Which of the following is less than $g(2)$?

    (A) $g(-3)$
    (B) $g(-1)$
    (C) $g(0)$
    (D) $g(3)$

15. If $b = 5a^3 - 2a + 7$ and $c = 2a^2 + a + 3$, what is $3c - b$ in terms of a ?

    (A) $-5a^3 + 6a^2 + a + 16$
    (B) $-5a^3 + 6a^2 + 3a - 4$
    (C) $-5a^3 + 6a^2 + 5a + 2$
    (D) $a^2 + 5a + 2$

$$x^2 - 2x = 7$$

16. * In the quadratic equation above, find the positive solution for x to the nearest tenth.

LEVEL 4: ADVANCED MATH

x	$p(x)$	$q(x)$	$r(x)$
-2	-3	4	-3
-1	2	1	2
0	5	-1	-6
1	-7	0	-5

17. The functions p, q and r are defined for all values of x, and certain values of those functions are given in the table above. What is the value of $p(-2) + q(0) - r(1)$?

18. Let the function f be defined for all values of x by $f(x) = x(x + 1)$. If k is a positive number and $f(k + 6) = 90$, what is the value of k?

x	-2	0	2
$f(x)$	$\dfrac{3}{25}$	3	75

19. The table above shows some values for the function f. If $f(x) = ab^x$ for some positive constants a and b, what is the value of b?

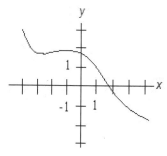

20. What is the maximum value of the function graphed on the xy-plane above, for $-4 \le x \le 4$?

    (A) -4
    (B) 3
    (C) 4
    (D) ∞

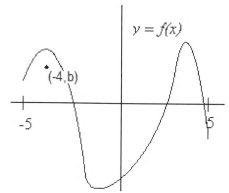

21. The figure above shows the graph of the function f and the point $(-4, b)$. For how many values of x between -5 and 5 does $f(x) = b$?

181

$$(x - 16)(x - n) = x^2 - 9nx + k$$

22. In the equation above, n and k are constants. If the equation is true for all values of x, what is the value of k ?

23. In the equation $x^2 - bx + c = 0$, b and c are integers. The solutions of this equation are 2 and 3. What is $c - b$?

LEVEL 5: ADVANCED MATH

$$x^2 + 2x - 1$$
$$2x^2 - x + 3$$

24. The product of the two polynomials shown above can be written in the form $ax^4 + bx^3 + cx^2 + dx + e$. What is the value of $\frac{b}{d}$?

Answers

1. 4	9. 3	17. 1
2. 10	10. 11	18. 3
3. 35	11. 4	19. 5
4. 3	12. 2	20. B
5. C	13. 22	21. 4
6. 6	14. D	22. 32
7. C	15. C	23. 1
8. 14	16. 3.8	24. 3/7, .428, or .429

LESSON 28
PROBLEM SOLVING AND DATA ANALYSIS

Try to solve each of the following problems. The answers to these problems are at the end of this lesson.

Full solutions to these problems are available for free download here:
www.thesatmathprep.com/28Les400.html

LEVEL 1: PROBLEM SOLVING AND DATA

1. The average (arithmetic mean) of ten numbers is 70. If the sum of nine of the numbers is 500, what is the tenth number?

2. For which of the following lists of 5 numbers is the average (arithmetic mean) less than the median?

    (A) 3, 3, 5, 6, 6
    (B) 3, 4, 5, 7, 8
    (C) 3, 3, 5, 7, 7
    (D) 3, 4, 5, 6, 7

3. Joe, Mike, Phil, and John own a total of 137 CDs. If John owns 38 of them, what is the average (arithmetic mean) number of CDs owned by Joe, Mike, and Phil?

4. If x is 22% of z and y is 37% of z, what is $x + y$ in terms of z?

    (A) $.15z$
    (B) $.43z$
    (C) $.59z$
    (D) $.81z$

5. The sales tax on a $7.50 scarf is $0.60. At this rate what would be the sales tax on a $12.00 scarf? (Disregard the dollar sign when gridding in your answer.)

6. The ratio of 29 to 5 is equal to the ratio of 203 to what number?

7. A copy machine makes 1800 copies per hour. At this rate, in how many <u>minutes</u> can the copy machine produce 3000 copies?

LEVEL 2: PROBLEM SOLVING AND DATA

8. The average (arithmetic mean) of 32, 60, and y is 60. What is the value of y ?

9. A is a set of numbers whose average (arithmetic mean) is 15. B is a set that is generated by multiplying each number in A by six. What is the average of the numbers in set B ?

10. The average (arithmetic mean) of seven numbers is 260. If an eighth number, 84, is added to the group, what is the average of the eight numbers?

$$15, 17, 3, 19, 2, 5, 22, 36, b$$

11. If b is the median of the 9 numbers listed above, which of the following could be the value of b ?

    (A) 4
    (B) 8
    (C) 14
    (D) 16

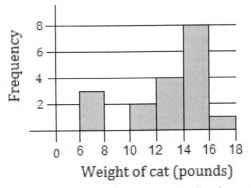

Weight of cat (pounds)

12. The histogram above shows the distribution of the weights, in pounds, of 18 cats in a shelter. Which of the following could be the median weight of the 18 cats represented in the histogram?

    (A) 10 pounds
    (B) 11 pounds
    (C) 13.5 pounds
    (D) 16 pounds

184

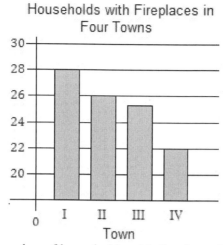

Households with Fireplaces in Four Towns

13. * The number of households with fireplaces in 4 towns is shown in the graph above. If the total number of such households is 10,150, what is an appropriate label for the vertical axis of the graph?

(A) Number of households with fireplaces (in tens)
(B) Number of households with fireplaces (in hundreds)
(C) Number of households with fireplaces (in thousands)
(D) Number of households with fireplaces (in tens of thousands)

14. On planet Puro, if each month has 12 days and each day has 8 hours, how many full Puro months will have passed after 400 hours?

(A) Two
(B) Three
(C) Four
(D) Five

LEVEL 3: PROBLEM SOLVING AND DATA

15. The average of x, y, z, and w is 16 and the average of z and w is 9. What is the average of x and y?

16. While observing several animals in a park, John notices that the rabbit is both the 6th largest and 6th smallest animal. If every animal that John observed was a different size, how many animals did John observe?

185

17. What percent of 75 is 32? (Disregard the percent symbol when gridding in your answer.)

18. During a sale at a music store, if a customer buys one CD at full price, the customer is given a 60 percent discount on a second CD of equal or lesser value. If John buys two CDs that have full prices of $15 and $25, by what percent is the total cost of the two CDs reduced during the sale? (Disregard the percent symbol when you grid your answer.)

19. * What is one possible value of x for which $\frac{6}{19} < x < \frac{1}{3}$?

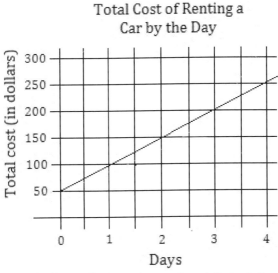

Total Cost of Renting a
Car by the Day

20. The graph above displays the total cost C, in dollars, of renting a car for d days. What does the C-intercept represent in the graph?

(A) The total number of days the cars is rented
(B) The total number of cars rented
(C) The initial cost of renting the car
(D) The increase in cost to rent the car for each additional day

186

21. Which of the following graphs best shows a strong positive association between x and y ?

(A)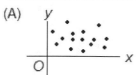

(B)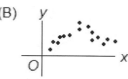

(C)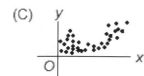

(D)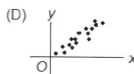

22. Daniel is drawing a time line to represent a 1000-year period of time. If he makes the time line 75 inches long and draws it to scale, how many inches will represent 80 years?

23. The ratio of the number of boys to the number of girls in a park is 5 to 11. What percent of the children in the park are girls?

   (A) 12.5%
   (B) 37.5%
   (C) 62.5%
   (D) 68.75%

LEVEL 4: PROBLEM SOLVING AND DATA

24. The average (arithmetic mean) of 7 numbers is j. If one of the numbers is k, what is the average of the remaining 6 numbers in terms of j and k?

   (A) $7j + k$
   (B) $\dfrac{6j - k}{7}$
   (C) $\dfrac{7j - k}{6}$
   (D) $\dfrac{7k - j}{6}$

187

Answers

1. 200
2. A
3. 33
4. C
5. .96
6. 35
7. 100
8. 88

9. 90
10. 238
11. D
12. C
13. B
14. C
15. 23
16. 11

17. 42.6 or 42.7
18. 45/2 or 22.5
19. .315 < x < .334
20. C
21. D
22. 6
23. D
24. C

ongratulations! By completing the lessons in this book, you have given yourself a significant advantage in SAT math. Go ahead and take a practice SAT. The math score you get should be much higher than the score you received before completing these lessons.

If you found that you were still getting many problems wrong in the last four lessons, this means that you can still show improvement by going through this book again. You can also use these last four lessons to determine exactly what you need more practice in. For example, if you got all the questions correct in Lesson 25 (Heart of Algebra), then there is no need to review the Heart of Algebra lessons in this book. But if you found, for example, that you got some questions wrong in Lesson 26 (Geometry), you may want to spend the next week or so redoing all the Geometry lessons from this book.

If you feel fairly confident with the questions from Lessons 25 through 28, then it is time to move on to the intermediate book in this series. The intermediate book can take you past a 700 in SAT math.

If you decide to use different materials for practice problems, please remember to try to solve each problem that you attempt in more than one way. Remember – the actual answer is not very important. What is important is to learn as many techniques as possible. This is the best way to simultaneously increase your current score, and increase your level of mathematical maturity.

I really want to thank you for putting your trust in me and my materials, and I want to assure you that you have made excellent use of your time by studying with this book. I wish you the best of luck on the SAT, on getting into your choice college, and in life.

Steve Warner, Ph.D.
steve@SATPrepGet800.com

ACTIONS TO COMPLETE AFTER YOU HAVE READ THIS BOOK

1. Take another practice SAT

You should see a substantial improvement in your score.

2. Continue to practice SAT math problems for 10 to 20 minutes each day

You may want to purchase *New SAT Math Problems arranged by Topic and Difficulty Level* for additional practice problems.

3. 'Like' my Facebook page

This page is updated regularly with SAT prep advice, tips, tricks, strategies, and practice problems. Visit the following webpage and click the 'like' button.

www.facebook.com/SATPrepGet800

4. Review this book

If this book helped you, please post your positive feedback on the site you purchased it from; e.g. Amazon, Barnes and Noble, etc.

5. Claim your FREE bonuses

If you have not done so yet, visit the following webpage and enter your email address to receive solutions to all the supplemental problems in this book and other materials.

www.thesatmathprep.com/28Les400.html

About the Author

Dr. Steve Warner, a New York native, earned his Ph.D. at Rutgers University in Pure Mathematics in May, 2001. While a graduate student, Dr. Warner won the TA Teaching Excellence Award.

After Rutgers, Dr. Warner joined the Penn State Mathematics Department as an Assistant Professor. In September, 2002, Dr. Warner returned to New York to accept an Assistant Professor position at Hofstra University. By September 2007, Dr. Warner had received tenure and was promoted to Associate Professor. He has taught undergraduate and graduate courses in Precalculus, Calculus, Linear Algebra, Differential Equations, Mathematical Logic, Set Theory and Abstract Algebra.

Over that time, Dr. Warner participated in a five-year NSF grant, "The MSTP Project," to study and improve mathematics and science curriculum in poorly performing junior high schools. He also published several articles in scholarly journals, specifically on Mathematical Logic.

Dr. Warner has more than 15 years of experience in general math tutoring and tutoring for standardized tests such as the SAT, ACT and AP Calculus exams. He has tutored students both individually and in group settings.

In February, 2010 Dr. Warner released his first SAT prep book "The 32 Most Effective SAT Math Strategies," and in 2012 founded Get 800 Test Prep. Since then Dr. Warner has written books for the SAT, ACT, SAT Math Subject Tests and AP Calculus exams.

Dr. Steve Warner can be reached at

steve@SATPrepGet800.com

BOOKS BY DR. STEVE WARNER

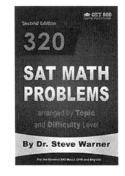

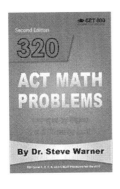
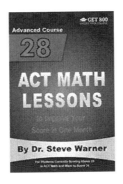
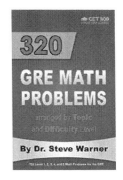

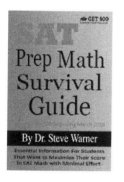

Made in the USA
Middletown, DE
27 March 2019